BREAN DOWN HARBOUR,
WESTON-SUPER-MARE, SOMERSET.

BREAN, THE MILLENNIUM YEARS

JOAN JACKMAN

A SQUARE ONE PUBLICATION

First published in Great Britain in 1999 by
Square One Publications
The Tudor House, 16 Church Street,
Upton on Severn, Worcestershire WR8 0HT

© 1999 Joan Jackman

ISBN: 1 8999 55 40 2

British Library Cataloguing in Publication Data is
available for this book

Typeset by Avon Dataset Ltd, Bidford on Avon B50 4JH

Printed in Great Britain by Biddles Ltd, Guildford, England

ACKNOWLEDGEMENTS

This has been a true village project. So many people have come forward with old newspaper cuttings, photographs and above all *memories*.

Evelyn Bagg, John Bailey – via his daughter Jill, Betty Board and brother Phil Champion, Mr & Mrs Clark, John Gearing and his son Ian for their Church Photography, Hugh Harris and Jonathon, Stuart Hicks, Donald and Bert House, Mrs Kent – an article by Mrs Naish, Mike Matthews, Daphne Price – for the use of Charles' research and writings, Walter Rowley, Irene Sampson, The Scott family, Mary Snook – her illustrations, Beth Strong, John Tucker, John Vowles, Martin Vowles, Evelyn Wormald.

Special thanks to Jo Wanford who typed it all, and who struggled with my handwriting and changes of mind and her 'cut and paste and insert technique' on her new computer.

My apologies to those people I've forgotten but who added the bits and pieces which filled in the gaps in my story.

V Joan Jackman, 1999

BREAN — THE MILLENNIUM YEARS

Brean Parish Council in the year 2000 presents one copy of this book to each household in Brean as a Millennium gift.

All profits from sales of the remaining copies will go to Village charitable causes.

Our thanks to the 'Awards for All' Lottery funding which has awarded £4,100 to Brean Residents Association to help fund this project.

CONTENTS

THE VILLAGE OF BREAN

Brean in the County of Somerset lies on the shores of the longest and largest inlet in England's coastline, the Bristol Channel, which separates the West of England from South Wales.

The channel is governed by the second largest rise and fall of tidal movement in the world (the greatest being in the Bay of Fundy in Canada).

The normal tides at Brean have a range of about 1 mile.

The Northernmost boundary is Brean Down, a rocky promontory jutting out into the channel and separating Brean from Weston-super-Mare which, for a short time, suffered the ignominy of being in the new County of Avon, but has now returned to Somerset. The River Axe rises in Wookey Hole and flows across the moors to its mouth in the Bristol Channel separating Brean Down from Weston and from the Mendip chain. A small ferry used to run across the Axe from Brean to Weston and back.

Brean Down is an extension of the Mendip Hills and is of the same carboniferous limestone formation as are the offshore islands of Flat Holm and Steep Holm. At one time the Down must have been an extension of the Mendip Hills, but rising sea levels about 5,000 BC flooded most of the surrounding land and made it an island. The Down dominates the Northern end of the village, on it are found signs of an ancient settlement with a history dating back 4,000 years to the Stone Age. Archaeological studies have found evidence of extinct mammoths, deer, bison and reindeer dating 10,000 years B.C. and burial mounds of the Bronze Age. Many interesting fossils have been found on the Down.

The South side of the Down is of steep cliffs with exposed limestone, but at the eastern end sand and sediment have built up over thousands of years in an area known as Sand Cliff, where most of the pre-historic bones have been found. It is likely that man hunted here when the Down was still part of the Mendips, but rising sea levels turned the surrounding area into a marshland.

As the waters receded, small communities settled and burial mounds have been found dating from the Bronze Age. Small

1

settlements such as these huddled together for safety as hill forts.

Excavation in 1976 by Dr Martin Bell of Lampeter University found the footings of round stone houses, bones and pottery out in the flat land some 100–200 metres from the shore, showing that the sea level was lower in the Bronze Age, and possibly this was the site of the original village of Brean.

Dr Martin Bell was guest speaker at Brean Parish Council's AGM of 1987 and gave an interesting account of archaeological 'Digs' on Brean Down. Many different discoveries have been made in the numerous 'layers' of the Down which have been investigated.

The top layer, dated as 5th/7th century, have revealed 5 Christian type burials, whilst 4 other layers found evidence of Bronze Age occupation, early Bronze Age and the Beaker Folk (a round-headed, heavy browed, square-jawed people who appeared in Britain at the start of the bronze Age. They were makers of round barrows in which bell-shaped pottery beakers are to be found.)

The earliest layer uncovered was approximately 2700 years BC after the Ice Age. Gold, copper and shell bracelets were discovered; they are now in Taunton Museum. It is thought that at one time people living on the Down were involved in salt production, which they used for trading purposes. The gold for ornamentation came from Ireland and large amounts of pottery and bone objects were discovered. The earliest findings on the Down were at the beginning of the century by Arthur Sarman, which were skulls. The greatest number of finds has been on the red sandstone slope which, by constant disturbance by man and animal, have had a constantly shifting surface. (It was a favourite place for children to slide, very dangerous as was proven by a Boy Scout killed there a few years ago, and buried by a cliff fall). Numerous animals, badgers, goats and rabbits have also scraped the surface and revealed traces of earlier cultures.

THE ROMAN TEMPLE

In 43 AD the Romans invaded Britain and set up trading posts for export. Local stone was exported, there was a quarry on Brean

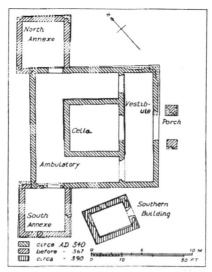

Brean Down Roman temple: plan showing building periods.
Vestibule – the forecourt or entry hall. *Cella* – the inner chamber of a
temple. *Ambulatory* – covered walkway.

A postcard of model of Roman Temple.

3

Down, and stone from here was used in the construction of a Roman Temple, which was excavated by Dr ApSimon of Bristol University in 1964/5. It is thought this temple was built towards the end of the Roman occupation, and may have been erected to a Deity of the River, it dates from about 340 AD and was then not of sufficient size and annexes were added. The original building was of local carboniferous limestone and of Bath freestone, possibly brought by water down the Avon and the Axe. The later buildings were not of as high a standard of building, decorating or material used, this was Dolomitic Conglomerate from the Mendips and Yellow Triassic from Bleadon.

Later the temple showed a period of dilapidation and then of occupancy by a nonreligious group. Signs of this occupation are of a cooking hearth in the vestibule and a blacksmith's workings in the North annexe.

Treasure seekers were then at work, robbers searching the abandoned temple and pits were dug under the cella hoping to find lost wealth. Coins have been found on the site but it is thought that these coins, when found, were useless and were left in disgust. Gold coins have also been found when quarrymen were taking off turf before digging for stone. Roman coins of Augustus, Nero and Drusus were found. Augustus was the nephew and successor to Julius Caesar.

The Southern building shows signs of domestic occupation, built later than the temple, probably 390 AD. Remains of shellfish and animal bones were discovered, signs of fishing and hunting. Spindle whorls were found indicative of domestic spinning probably to make the inhabitants' clothing. Human remains were found in the North annexe, possibly the inhabitant of the Southern building. Some of the stone used for building the southern part came from the original temple after its destruction.

THE DARK AGES

Little is known of Brean in the Dark Ages, but the earliest signs of Christianity are from burial mounds on the South side of the

Down excavated in 1989 and carbon dated as being 410 AD, before Christian religion was found at Wells or Glastonbury. The first mention of rabbits, or conies, as they were known is in the reign of Henry II, 1145–89. They may have been brought by soldiers returning from the Crusades. One of the earliest documented rabbit warrens was on the Down which was practically an island and, with no other predators, they multiplied and were hunted and sold for their meat and fur, and formed a staple part of the diet.

After 878 AD Monasteries were established at Glastonbury and Athelney, and the monks did much to improve land drainage.

Little changed in Brean in the Middle Ages. As drainage schemes improved in the flat lands adjoining the Down, the land was improved for agriculture, sheep were grazed. On the Down itself there is evidence firstly of Celtic field systems with raised grass covered banks.

Much sea defence work was done, land was reclaimed from the sea, brushwood, stakes and low walls were built and a thick vegetation encouraged to cover the mud and reclaimed land. The sea wall South of the Axe can be seen today and further sea defences are still being carried out there. Drainage ditches, known as Rhines, were dug extensively.

THE DOMESDAY BOOK

In 1066 William of Normandy conquered England – a date most people remember, but little more about it. In 1085 Domesday Book, so called 'The Day of Judgment', was compiled. Men were sent all over England to find out what was held by whom and what it was worth. The survey was completed very rapidly and, in some places, double-checked by Commissioners to check and report to the King if anyone were cheating. The survey was completed in 12 months and then written up in the great book, so that the King would know his land and the landowners their rights.

Somerset was given to one of William's favoured Knights, Walter de Douai (or Dowai in some versions), and Domesday records, 'Walter himself holds BRIEN', and after this various Lords owned Brean, though it is unlikely that any of them lived there, but would have derived rents from the farmers who were tenants. Domesday describes Brien as having 'land for 8 plough-teams, 1 hide in the demesne and 3 plough-teams, 9 villeins, 3 cottard, 10 beasts, 4 swine, 53 sheep and 30 acres of pasture – worth 100 shillings for tax.' (A hide was a land unit reckoned at 120 acres. A villein or servant was not allowed to leave his native village). Walter must have been a considerable landowner since he was given Burnham and Brean.

By the thirteenth century the Brean Church of Saint Bridget had been dedicated. This indicates an early Celtic Christian settlement, which settlements were nearly always in coastal areas, the Irish monks being unwilling to travel far inland, preferring a navigable river or safe sea escape route, and these were also valuable trading routes.

Brean Down Farm is probably the oldest farm in the village. Whilst some of its building is nineteenth century, other parts have walls 6 feet thick which suggests that, at one time, it was part of a medieval fort, and other farmhouses in the village, though later in construction, were on medieval fort sites.

THE DISSOLUTION OF THE MONASTERIES

Henry VIII came to the throne in 1509, and in 1536 started the dissolution of the monasteries. In 1539 Glastonbury Abbey was dissolved and the last Abbot hung on the Tor.

By 1593 the lands had passed into the hands of small land-owners and absentee Lords, who were not interested in land drainage, building sea walls, or development, so in 1607, when the worst flood came, Brean was under water. Of the nine houses which are recorded as forming the village, seven were destroyed. In places surrounding villages were flooded to a depth of 10 to 12 feet, many people lost their lives and Brean is recorded as having lost 26 people. Major floods occurred in 1703, 1859, 1903, 1910 and 1926.

The high rise and fall of the tides and high Spring and Autumn tides brought much suspended vegetable matter to the wetlands, and during low tides, reclamation work on the land could be made. During 1620–40 land south of the Axe was reclaimed for Brean.

Rabbits were such a valuable commodity that artificial rabbit warrens were created and young rabbits put into them to encourage them to breed, and remains of these warrens are now called 'Pillow Mounds' by archaeologists and a number have been identified on Brean Down.

Rabbit keeping and subsequent selling of the carcasses and the fur was a very profitable business, as well as the rabbits being a very valuable addition to the diet. Weston Library has a cutting from a 1919 scrapbook giving the history of a court case which was taken to the Star Chamber for settlement.

Thomas Bond of London owned the ancient Brean Down Rabbit Warren, being 400 acres in size and adjoining the sea side (from the size given this must be far greater that the Down itself, and probably was the land now Warren Road). He employed two men to attend the warren and grounds. They had a dwelling place and storage for nets, ferrets, dogs and weapons.

The warreners had to guard against poachers who might well be armed and vicious. One Friday night in 1607 the warreners were awakened by noises from the Warren. When they went to investigate they found ten men armed with shafts, daggers and pistols, who had forced their way into the enclosure and had hunted and killed forty rabbits. When they confronted the thieves they were insulted and attacked physically.

Nicholas Battersby of Uphill was taken before the Star Chamber and accused of the crime. Unfortunately the findings of the court are not given. But the absentee landlord – owner of the land, Thomas Bond, sold out in 1637 to Henry Lord Danvers and Anthony Garrard, and we know that they too sold out in 1883 to William Wyndham.

THE NINETEENTH CENTURY

During the Nineteenth Century further progress was made in reclaiming the land. Stakes, hedges and brushwood helped to stabilise it, suspended vegetation in the mud and silt from high tides was deposited, and other vegetation developed. A system of ditches or rhines helped to drain the land, and the Clyse was constructed at Hobbs Boat on the Weston road where pressure doors allowed flood water to go out to sea but prevented salt water from flooding inland.

For centuries the land on the seaside had never been built on and, though belonging to the manor, could be used by villagers to graze sheep. The land was mainly of blown sand, difficult to cultivate, because the strong prevailing wind from the sea being salt laden, killed most vegetation. In 1742 an Act of Parliament ordered that sand sedge should be planted at Berrow to help stabilise the dunes.

THE WYNDHAM CONNECTION

After the land of Brien had been granted to Walter of Douai, who also owned much of other parts of the West of England, many others succeeded him as Lord of the Manor. Like the Rectors of Breane, few of the Lords lived in the village which was a small poor place but, as part of the feudal system of England, the landowner of the Manor could extract rents from the tenants, so the Lords became wealthy without putting anything back into the land they owned, and the serfs tilled and worked the land to increase the riches of the Lords.

Thus Brean passed from generation to generation either by inheritance or sale. In 1637 the land was sold in two portions, the Lord of the Manor at that time sold one portion to Henry Lord Danvers and Anthony Garrard, which was obviously the north end of Brean – 'The Down or Warren called Brean Down and the newly built Brean Down Farmhouse'. The second portion was sold to William Cann of Bristol and his heirs, and much of this appears to be the coastal strip since it included sea wrecks, fishing rights, royalties and rents. In 1795 he is recorded as having sold a parcel of his land to Samuel Hix. The Hicks family had rented farm land since 1730, and this might be the first land bought.

The first portion of land, passed in 1883 to William Wyndham, who though called Lord of the Manor lived at Dinton, Salisbury. His family were large Somerset landowners and played a part in much of the history of the County. He is listed as being one of the subscribers towards the restoration of St. Bridget's Church for the sum of £50 in 1883, when Rev T W Strong set in motion the restoration of the Church.

At this time Brean Parish covered an area of 1,167 acres in a part of Somerset called Brent Marsh, the land being divided between eight farms and 24 acres of Glebe land. Again many names listed in Kelly's Directory of 1889 are familiar:

> Jeffery Cox, farmer Diamond Farm.
> Thomas Curry, The Manor Farm. Edward Dibble, Upper Farm.
> Jas. Frith, Brean Down Farm. Philip Harris, Warren Farm.
> Edmund Hicks – farmer. Henry Adams Hicks – farmer.
> Enoch & Frederick Sperring – Turnbourne Farm.

William Wyndham sold off portions of land to various farmers which was sold by the acre, and included the dune land and onto the sea shore to the mean high tide line. (The line of average height between the highest and lowest tide mark). This dune land was of little value. It consisted of blown sand, tunnelled by rabbit burrows (there seem to have been few foxes then), and many Shelduck which nested in the burrows and hence were called Burrow Ducks or Barrow Ducks.

THE RIVER AXE

The Eastern boundary of Brean is the tidal River Axe, It's source is Wookey Hole and until the Nineteenth Century this was a busy shipping highway, and on high tides ships could travel as far as Rackley.

The Romans certainly used the Axe and had a port on the river. We don't know the name of this port but Doomsday Book calls it Opopille. Pill means a creek or harbour. Possibly the name Hobbs Boat comes from the Danish pirate Hubba, who fought King Alfred close by the Polden Hills.

In the Middle Ages water transport was preferable to travel on the narrow rutted English country roads. At one time the River Brue and River Axe were connected by the Pillrow Cut, so that the Abbott of Glastonbury could visit all his lands by boat (the Pillrow Cut is shown these days as the Mark Yeo).

Iron, salt, wine from Lisbon, oil, vinegar and wax from Bayonne, France, were cargoes sent up river to the port of Rackley near Crook Peak. Then they were transported by barges, which would take the cargo on waterways to Wells. From Somerset corn and woollen goods were sent back to Portugal and France.

The flow of water in the Axe, fresh water from Wookey and tidal waters from Brean caused many acres of flood land. In 1795 John Billingsley, a farmer from Shepton Mallett, was one of the prime movers in a review of agricultural land in Somerset. He proposed that a barrier with sluice gates across the Axe would stop this flooding. The Commission of Sewers opposed this because they did not want navigation on the Axe to end, but the land owners suffered unusually bad flooding in the winter of 1799 and applied for an Act of Parliament to build sluice gates. They obtained this in 1802 and the gates at Hobbs Boat were agreed. The work was completed in 1810, which not only improved the drainage of the low lands, but also eliminated the large amount of stagnant water which used to collect.

(The Commission of Sewers was established in 1304 requiring people to perform certain drainage duties, clearing of rhines etc. with heavy penalties for those who neglected their duties).

After the construction of the sluice gate at Hobbs Boat, ships ceased going to the port of Rackley and, with no port, the village became only a smattering of a few houses.

Coal continued to be delivered by boat, but went only as far as the coal wharf at Lympsham. Coal for Weston and Brean was collected by horse and wagon from the wharf which was owned and run by Mr Jones and his son Tom. The railway line ran across here at Brean Halt, so boats could go no further.

The Commission of Sewers by this time was called 'Rhine Viewers'. Small sluices existed at all the main farms, Warren, Diamond, Tuckers at Brean Farm, Southfield and, when the tide came in, they shut automatically. But these gates, the coal wharf sluice and Hobbs Boat were getting old and began to leak, so in 1970 new gates at Diamond Farm Sluice were installed and became the one main outlet.

By this time rhine control was under the ruling of the Somerset Drainage Board and no major floods have occurred in recent years, since drainage of the land can be controlled by the opening and closing of sluice gates and raising or lowering of water level in the rhines. Rhine levels are therefore controlled by members of the Drainage Board. They contain fresh water, an example of a rhine is the waterway running alongside Red Road, but ditches such as run alongside the old Weston Road, are the responsibility of the farmer who owns the land, and they contain stagnant water. The Drainage Board has to clear and clean the rhines once or twice a year, the farmers are responsible for their ditches.

LIMESTONE QUARRIES

Quarry workings on Brean Down are evident from many years ago. It would appear that some of the stone used in building the Roman Temple is of carboniferous limestone quarried from the Down. Many of the Brean farmhouses contain very thick walls probably of stone quarried locally.

A letter from Jesse Hawkings, farmer at Brean Down Farm, berates Axbridge District Council for using stone transported from Bleadon to mend Brean roads when it was always the custom to use local stone.

Brean roads were narrow and rutted and made up of rough stone broken small by Daniel Durston and his son Phillip. The stone was brought from the quarry on the Down in big pieces, by horse and cart, and laid by the roadside to be rolled in by steamroller. Most of the farmers kept their own roads in repair. Men and women alike needed to wear tough boots to walk Brean roads, otherwise the sharp stones cut through.

Stone was carried by sea to Bridgwater and Minehead. Quarrying on the Down ceased when Axbridge RDC purchased it.

SALT MAKING

There is evidence that Brean was one of the earliest known sites for salt making. It is not known which method was used for this process. It is possible that salt water was collected in summer time from the sea and then evaporated out in the sun. Summer is the time of highest salinity of the sea at Brean, because in Winter the salt water is diluted by increased river water. Alternatively, salt may have been processed by being heated in a briquetage over a slow burning fire, probably fuelled by peat. This was a brick shaped tray and salt cakes formed in it, then they could be traded still in the clay covering or this was broken and the salt cake removed.

There are signs of a hearth in the southern part of the temple, so it is possible that salt water was collected from the sea, carried back up the Down and the briquetage method used. Salt was a valuable trading commodity, and might have been traded for pottery or ornaments.

THE BREAN DOWN FERRY

The last river ferry in Somerset ran from the foot of Brean Down across the River Axe to Uphill, Weston-super-Mare.

Actual recorded history of the ferry is from 1637 when, in the deeds of Brean Manor, the ferry is part of the land owned by the Lord of the Manor. Reference is made to a newly built house (Brean Down Farm), 400 acres of land including the down or warren and the ferry.

Certainly the Romans, soldiers, worshippers at the temple and river traders must have used a crossing, but no actual ferry is recorded.

When the sluice gates at Hobbs Boat opened in 1810, the ferry at Brean Down was not used for some years but, as Weston-super-Mare developed, so the wish to visit Brean Down increased. In 1808 Weston's first hotel opened, and pleasure boats and steam packets ran from Weston.

Irene Sampson, in her story as a waitress at Brean Down Café, recalls how, once a week, she went across on the ferry for supplies from Weston and, in the 1920's, it is recorded that up to 700

THE FERRY, BREAN, WESTON-SUPER-MARE

people a day used the ferry to take day trips to the Down. The daughters of Roland Frost at Brean Down Farm used to be taken across on the ferry to school at Uphill.

On Bank Holidays 2 motor boats and a row-boat were in operation, run by the ferryman, A E Pople. At low tide 3 boats were tied together and people could walk across from boat to boat.

In summer the ferry ran from 9.30 am – 5.00 pm, but in winter you had to write to Mr Pople and book an appointment. When Mr Pople died, the ferry was sold to Captain Smart for £30. He was a merchant seaman who had travelled the world and looked the part, with red face, white moustache, gold earrings and navy jersey and cap. He got into trouble with local fishermen because he refused to allow the ferry boat landing stages at Uphill to be used, claiming he owned both the Brean and Uphill stages. The case was taken to court and Captain Smart lost the case, Uphill Parish Council's claim that it was a public landing area being upheld, and he had to allow the fisherman to use it.

During the war Brean Down was closed to the public and, in 1951, Captain Smart's daughter, Mary, sold out at auction to a Weston lifeboatman for the paltry sum of £6.00. But he had not got a bargain. The service became very irregular, people went by car to Brean, there was no café at the end of the Down, but the convenient Cove Café and the Bird Garden were at the foot, with car parking space and few used or even knew of the ferry.

In 1975 'Gordon the Ferryman' took over but he too clashed with Woodspring Council who declared his operation illegal. He and his ferry were uninsured and safety regulations were flouted, and so the ferry closed again.

ST BRIDGET'S CHURCH, BREANE

St Bridget's Church probably dates from the thirteenth century, named after St Bridget, Abbess of Kildare in Ireland who died in 525 AD Her dedication here is an indication of very early Celtic Christian settlement. Such settlements with links to Wales and

Rev E A H Strong, outside Breane Church.

Ireland were coastal settlements from which escape by sea was possible in time of trouble and good areas for trading.

Pope Nicholas IV, between 1288–91, made an assessment of all Churches with a view to taxing them. Brean was obviously reckoned a poor Church, taxed only at £2.00.

It is possible that the early Brean Church was a wooden structure, but in the 1300's many of Somerset's Churches were re-built, and it is thought that much of the stonework of St Bridget's dates from this time.

The Rectory at Brean in 1535 was valued at £7.0.4 at a time when Henry VII ordered a valuation of all the Churches in the country, and by 1668 at £30.00. Brean Church has suffered from storm and neglect and, being in a poor and sparsely populated parish, was never able to have much money spent on its main-tenance. The three bells in the tower date from about 1500; they are inscribed Sancta Micail (Saint Michael), Deus Sancta Virgo Maria (God out of the Virgin Mary) and Sancta Dionisi ora pro

Top left: St Bridget's Church – The Jacobean Pulpit. 'George Gudrid gave this in 1620'.

Top right: St Bridget's Church – The Lectern.

Above: St Bridget's Church – Oak bench stands in porch. Probably 600 years old.

Right: The Shamrock shaped Piscina.

nobis (Saint Dennis is praying for us.) They were probably cast about 1500 by a bell-founder whose initials were T G. The original pews were of oak thought to have been 600 years old, hewn into shape with an adze (a cutting tool with an arched blade used for cutting wood). One of the very old pews stands in the porch. The font is octagonal with flowers carved round the bowl. It is of thirteenth century origin. It is thought that at one time the font may have had a lock, this was often done so that the contents could not be stolen and used for witchcraft. The pulpit is Jacobean and carved between the panels 'George Gudrid gave this, 1620'. Still in use in the Church today is a silver Communion Cup given by William Hicks in 1756.

St Bridget's shows areas of restoration and neglect. The present perpendicular structure style is approximately fifteenth century, but the chancel was rebuilt in the nineteenth century. The floor was originally made of locally found rounded pebbles which were not replaced with the present tiles until 1890, when a period of restoration took place after years of neglect. When these pebbles were removed a number of skeletons were found underneath, lying close to the surface.

A great storm in 1729 destroyed the tower when it was struck by lightening. The village raised £60.9.6 to restore it, but though this was a considerable sum in those days, it was not sufficient to restore it to its old height and so the tower was shortened and given the saddle back roof which can be seen today. John Leech, a churchman who travelled the county writing accounts of his visits for Bristol newspapers, likened Brean Church 'to a dovecote'.

Church finances were maintained by a rate on all the houses in Brean, and villagers wanting to keep this low, spent only £3.2.0 on the Church in 1781 and £1.15 of this was the Parish Clerk's fee. Consequently the Church fell into a very bad state of repair, with broken pews and windows and little repair was undertaken until the 1880's.

There was a building North of the Church called by many inhabitants 'the dead house'. Bodies washed ashore from ship-wrecks were laid out in the dead house prior to inquest which was held in the Rectory itself.

Bodies washed ashore prior to 1837 were frequently merely buried in the sand above high water mark. But in 1837 compulsory registration of births and deaths became statutory and an inquest had to be held. It was also quite common that such bodies were not buried in consecrated ground since their religion was unknown.

There were many wrecks off Brean and the islands. In 1810 the cargo boat 'Rebecca', running from the West Indies to Bristol, lost her cargo of rum washed up at Brean, and a Spanish boat, the 'Anita', was lost in 1901 with all hands lost and wreckage and bodies washed up at Brean. From 280 wrecks around the United Kingdom coasts, 27 were in the Bristol Channel. The Rector in 1903 reported that in twenty years he had buried nine bodies of sailors. Inhabitants finding bodies washed up on the share were given a payment as reward. One such body, whose inquest was held at the Rectory, was examined by Dr Wade, and Reverend T W Strong was the foreman of the jury. The verdict given was 'found drowned', and the body is buried in the cemetery.

A small memorial was erected to show the graves of unknown sailors, erected in 1872, it is made of iron and inscribed;

> The cruel winds and yawning waves
> Hurried me to my doom
> While wife and children dear
> Waited for me at home.

Ten years after its positioning some mindless nineteenth century vandal removed the memorial and took it to the beach and used it for target practice. Since then it has been encased in stone and has been renovated and made more legible. Major restoration work was carried out in 1883 under the direction of Messrs Price & Wooler, Architects of Weston-super-Mare, when the chancel was rebuilt. The benches were renewed in oak and the bench ends in the nave copied from existing fragments of the old. An oak lych-gate was erected at the entrance to the churchyard which, in recent years, has had to be replaced using as much as possible of the original oak.

At the South side of the Church there was a vestry, which can be seen in old photographs of St Bridget's, this was demolished and not rebuilt at that time. The chancel too was demolished and rebuilt, much of which was paid for by the Reverend T Strong. When the chancel wall was broken down to make an entry from the vestry to the chancel, a very old archway and door was found. In the South wall of the chancel is an ancient piscina, a holy water drain in the shape of a shamrock seemingly showing the Church's Irish links.

Other money was raised by subscription, names still well known in the village appeared on the subscription list, Board, Harris, Hicks and Hobbs among them, and the restoration costs are listed as £459.9.8. One other contributor's name was that of the Church Warden, Mr William Sperring, who was not only a prime mover in getting the restoration work completed, but also did much physical work on the nave. In 1892 the Church was presented with a fine lectern in memory of William Sperring. In the cemetery today the Brean War Memorial reads:

> In memory of the Men who fell in the Great War
> 1914–1918
> Champion Ivor E.
> *Dibble George
> Evans Lot
> Giblett Sidney
> Phillips Medford
> Starbuck Richard
> Webb William   Men from Brean.

* Henry George Dibble – died in France on 11th April 1917 aged 20 years is buried with his parents at Brean.

RECTORS OF BREANE

—	John de Sarum	—	Ric Rowlandesonn
1318	Ric de Bocwell	1584	Thomas Wellsteede
1322	John Barbe	1596	Joh. Marshe
1332	William de Styntyscomb	1600	Ric. Mason
1334	Henry Russel	1613	Geo. Knibb
1351	Joh. Chaundos	1637	Nath. Conduit AM
1401	John Caume	1662	Francis Atkins
1402	John Smyth	1663	Roger Ley AM
1402	Ric. Wyke	1693	Edm. Stacey
—	Ric. Avery	1667	David Barnes
1419	John Talbot	1704	Sam Baker AB
1454	Hugo Sugar	1725	Benjamin Hancock AM
1460	Will Lyndesey	1765	Charles Willes MA
1462	Joh. Welyngton	1770	W T Bowles
1478	David Frampton	1787	W S Willies MA
1482	Tho. Barott	1789	Martin Stafford Smith BD
1498	Joh. Benett	1831	Edward Willes MA
1499	Tho. Birde	1849	Michael Terry BA
1504	Will Basset	1855	C W Devis MA
1523	Jac. Carter	1859	Joseph Halifax MA
1547	Joh. Lyll	1882	T W Strong MA
		1920	Ernest A H Strong

In 1972 the Rectors became Rectors of Berrow and Breane.

1972 Christopher Herbert Saralis MA
1976 William St. John Kemm MA
1992 Stafford Low BSc

THE RECTORS OF BREANE

The Historical Notes on St Bridget's Church, Breane, gives this list of the Rectors of Breane from the C14 to the present day. Few of these Rectors actually lived in Breane and, in fact, rarely visited it but paid a curate to take services there. The Rectors received a tithe or tenth of the produce of every crop or animal in the parish. The clergy too might own glebe land upon which they could grow crops or keep animals for their own profit. Thus a Rector might abide in a wealthy living where he preached, but receive tithes from several villages he had been granted.

The absenteeism among the clergy probably accounted for the bad state of disrepair which Breane Church was allowed to fall into, and the lack of book-keeping and of up-dating of the Church register.

In 1765 the patronage was bought by the Willes family, and three of the family became Rectors, 1765 Charles Willes, 1787 William Willes and 1831 Edward Willes. They did not live in Brean but kept the living as a valuable addition to their income. The first resident vicar was Michael Terry in 1849, who considerably enlarged the rectory, previously described by Martin Stafford-Smith in 1789 as 'a mean cottage, in very good repair but totally unfit for a clergyman' – but since he lived in Worcester and Bath and employed a curate, this did not matter greatly.

In 1882 the Rev Thomas Watson Strong MA became the resident Rector and proceeded to do a great deal to restore the Church. A new chancel was built and new seats put in. Sand had built up around the Church so that the floor level was 4 ft. below the surrounding level, and a moat had to be dug round the outside. The pebbled floor of the Church was replaced with a new tiled floor.

There were large holes in the roof so that the exposed timbers, which had been open to the rains and salt winds of Brean, were rotten. Two out of three windows had to be replaced and new pews were installed, a badly needed repair, since John Leech wrote in the 1840's. 'As I sat down on one of the "free" back seats intended for agricultural labourers and their children, the rotten board almost broke beneath my weight, although I am by no means ponderous'.

In 1883 the Church was rededicated at a service conducted by the Bishop of Bath and Wells and the Archdeacon. Restoration cost £600, much of which was donated by Rev Strong himself,

The Reverend & Mrs Thomas Strong – In the Rectory garden

but village efforts, bazaars and donations also contributed to the fund.

Thomas Watson Strong died in 1922 and was succeeded by his son, Revd Ernest Strong.

Rev Ernest Arthur Herbert Strong was a great character, well known, not only in Breane, (the Ecclesiastical spelling upon which he insisted), but in Church and sporting circles throughout the County.

Born in the Rectory in October 1883, he became a great rural enthusiast taking part in many rural pursuits and becoming a wildlife expert on the birds and plants of field and seashore. He went away to school at Uffculme, Lyme Regis, St. Dunstans at Burnham and All Hallows, Honiton. His clerical training was at the Theological College, Chichester where he obtained his MA. He was ordained in 1908, and in 1909 became a priest. He served in Cambridge, Honiton, and took over from his father, when he died, at Breane in 1920.

As a sportsman he was well known, having been a keen schoolboy cricketer and school captain, then playing for several local clubs. He was an enthusiastic follower of Somerset cricket and used to get to County matches whenever possible. He also played tennis and hockey, and, for many years, was a member of Burnham and Berrow Golf Club. There was a grass tennis court in the Rectory garden where he and his friends enjoyed a social game.

But his main sporting interest was as a life member of the Wild Fowlers' Association, and his living room walls were decorated with mounted heads of duck and teal. His living room at the rectory had to be seen to be believed. If you were invited to sit down, first you had to clear a chair of either books, papers or cats. (At one time he had 13 of these!). Then as you sat and talked, ducks or geese would wander in through the front door. The walls were lined with bookshelves – he is reputed to have a library of 5,000 books which reflected his vast interests through sport, wild life, animal husbandry and Penguin 'thrillers'. On his glebe land he kept pigs and cows, runner ducks, Chinese geese, and his special Light Sussex hens. The milk girl was rewarded with 2

Rev E A H Strong and 'Feathers'.

duck eggs to take home each week and the postman with fall down apples.

He grew most of his own vegetables and, after his wife Maude died, looked after himself with, in particular, a special and somewhat unappetising bowl of porridge, which he made, and with which he started each day.

Whilst he loved animals, they too loved him and, when he visited his younger son Dick, in Brent Knoll, he and his wife had a budgie called Feathers, which used to go crazy when 'Parson' arrived. He had to be let out of his cage and flew at once to settle on his bald head or snuggle up against his clerical collar for the evening. Revd Strong took an important part in village life and was Chairman of Brean Parish Council, Vice-Chairman of the Central Branch of the Somerset Association of Parish Councils, local representative of the Soldiers, Sailors and Airmen's Families Association, and local representative of the Somerset Rural Industries Council.

Brean & Berrow ARP

Back row standing: Gladys Coombe, John Tidball, Bill Thorne, George Gibbon, ? George Davis, Arthur Dibble, Walt Bishop, Rev E Strong, Mike Dunn, Fred Champion.
Middle row: Percy Priddy, Phil Durston, Jim Talbot, Dick Talbot, Fred Bryant, Jim Capel, Jim Kerton, Doug Capel, Fred Harris, Miss Brown.
Front row: Mrs Furness, Mrs Williams, Murial Tidball, Pam Betts, Mary Dunn, Reg Noyce, Christine Young, Ruth Johnson, Ciss Coome, Chickie Price, Miss Jeffries, Miss Jeffries.

During the war he was in the ARP (Air Raid Precaution) unit and spent many nights on fire watch duty. Surprisingly, many bombs were dropped on Brean, incendiaries possibly dumped after attacks on Cardiff or Bristol, or dropped because of the dummy airport lit up at Lympsham and sea mines also landed in the locality. He was a well-recognised figure in the village, with flannel bags held up by an old tie, trilby hat, gardening boots and a pipe clenched in his teeth, only a 'dog collar' telling him apart from an agricultural labourer. But his vast range of knowledge, erudite speech, humour and straight talk, set him aside from others, and he was a much loved and respected figure in the village.

At 90, in 1972, Revd. Strong retired and went to life with his son, John, at Marram Dune, opposite the Church and died aged 93. The Rectory was sold and became a private house and, in

1972, the Church had no resident vicar in Brean but shared with Berrow, the Revd C H Sarilis, being 'ic' the two parishes. This arrangement has continued with Rev W St John Kemm in 1976, and Rev Stafford Low in 1992.

THE START OF METHODISM IN BREAN

William Hicks, great, great, great grandfather of Stuart Hicks who still lives in Brean, farmed at Southfield Farm. Southfield has been occupied by the Hicks family since about 1700, and has been in the family ever since. The main farmhouse was probably built about 1760, but the original cottage was much earlier. It is believed that some part of the original building was surrounded and damaged by the floods of 1607 which swept miles inland. Nowadays Southfield Farm is a listed building. Newgate Prison existed not only in London but also in Bristol since 1148, being rebuilt in 1691, when it was described as 'white without and foul within'. Public hangings were

Tour of Southfield Farm
Austin Hicks, George Parsons, Arthur Sampson, 1937.

26

conducted at Newgate and William Hicks attended one of these, which totally disgusted and disturbed him.

That same day William heard John Wesley preach and, particularly after the scenes which he had witnessed earlier, was so impressed by Wesley's preaching that he invited him if he was ever in the vicinity of Brean to come and preach at Southfield Farm. This he did when visiting Brent Knoll in 1769. John Wesley used to ride on horseback over the countryside visiting, preaching and converting to Methodism. It is believed he preached in the living room at Southfield, staying the night and stabling his horse on the farm.

It has recently been recognised that Southfield Farm was the first Wesleyan Chapel in the Weston area and continued to be a chapel for 90 years from 1765–1847. In 1804 it was licensed to register marriages and baptisms. It is strange to note that, whilst the Hicks family held Methodist meetings at Southfield Farm, they still continued to be Church members and worshipped at St. Bridget's Brean, services being held so that, if Church was in the morning, the Chapel service was in the evening.

In 1847 Henry Adam Hicks lived at Southfield but, having eight children, needed the space of his living room and had no room to hold services there. The Hicks family owned 2 cottages (next to what is now the Post Office), and, whilst the one nearest the Down was a farm worker's cottage, the other became a Chapel. Though given to the community as a Wesleyan Methodist chapel, the Hicks family made as part of the agreement that, if at any time a new chapel were to be built, the land and buildings would revert to the family. This was done when the new chapel was built in 1933 and the houses are still owned by Stuart Hicks, the one being rented as a private dwelling, and the other used as a health and beauty salon. The first still bears the inscription, 'Wesleyan Chapel', and is now called Tween Cottage.

The little chapel in the cottage thrived and in 1851, when a census was made of chapels and churches in England and Wales, it is recorded by Henry G Hicks that there were 9 free seats and 4 rented, and 30 people attended evening service. In the morning, Church services were held in St Bridget's, where Henry was a

T'ween Cottage – Church Road. The old Wesleyan Chapel.

Churchwarden, and the Methodist service in the afternoon or evening. These services were often so full that the congregation had to stand and children frequently sat on the sandbank outside.

The present Methodist Chapel was opened in 1933 on land given by Henry Morse Hicks and Austin Hicks, much of the fund raising being done by Herbert Gillings. Brean Parish Council of 1972 presented the Methodist Church with a clock as an amenity for the village. This is mounted above the front door. It was made by John Smith & Co. of Derby, and is illuminated and designed to blend with the Church architecture. The clock was unveiled by Rev E A H Strong and Councillor J G Walter, Chairman of Axbridge Rural District Council who addressed the gathering. The Parish Council of 1972 was:

Chairman	Rev E A H Strong
Vice Chairman	S A F Hicks
	Mrs E Robbins
	B Rees
	E Allport
	R Sims
Clerk to the Council	A J Ham

Brean Parish Council

You are invited to attend
the

Unveiling of
the Parish Clock

—

at The Methodist Church, Brean
on Wednesday, 22nd November, 1972
at 7 p.m.

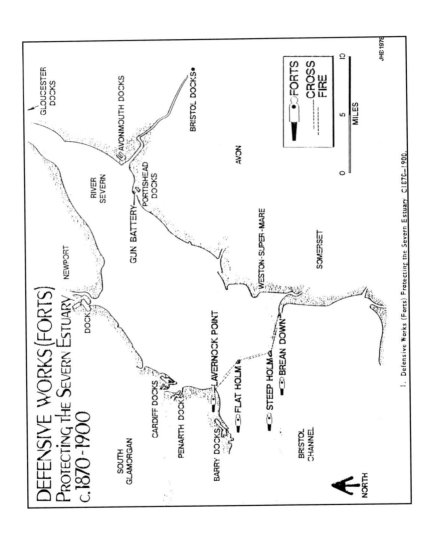

DEFENSIVE WORKS (FORTS)
PROTECTING THE SEVERN ESTUARY
c.1870-1900

GLOUCESTER DOCKS

AVONMOUTH DOCKS

BRISTOL DOCKS •

RIVER SEVERN

GUN BATTERY

PORTISHEAD DOCKS

AVON

WESTON-SUPER-MARE

SOMERSET

NEWPORT

DOCK

SOUTH GLAMORGAN

CARDIFF DOCKS

PENARTH DOCK

LAVERNOCK POINT

FLAT HOLM

STEEP HOLM

BREAN DOWN

BARRY DOCKS

BRISTOL CHANNEL

NORTH

FORTS

CROSS FIRE

MILES

0   5   10

JHE 1978

1. Defensive Works (Forts) Protecting the Severn Estuary C1870-1900.

THE MARITIME FORT OF BREAN DOWN

The brief Franco-Austrian war of 1859 spread fears of the growth of Napoleon III's aggressive intent and his building up of the French Navy and, in particular, his new steam driven battleships, spread fears among the British of the threat of war or invasion.

Lord Palmerston was anxious to increase arms expenditure, increase the fortifications of British coasts, improve old forts and build new. The Chancellor of the Exchequer, Gladstone, threatened to resign over the proposed expenditure, but in 1862 the Government announced that a Bristol Channel defence line had been approved.

As neither the threatened war nor invasion materialised, these became known as 'Palmerston's Follies', but did remain a strong deterrent.

These Victorian forts were built on the islands of Flat Holm and Steep Holm, on Lavernock Point on the Welsh side and on Brean Down. They were armed with 29 7inch Rifled Muzzle Loading (RML) guns. The same positions were used in the 2nd World War when Channel defences were again manned to defend

The Fort, Brean Down

31

the Welsh ports and Bristol, Avonmouth and Portishead.

By 1870–72 the fort on Brean Down was completed, and by 1873 a garrison of about 60 artillerymen occupied it. In 1881 it was inspected by a military sub-committee who commented that the battery was well placed and in an efficient state. Recruitment was difficult to man the Coast Brigade. Officers and men felt they were in a remote service, life was boring and, particularly on the Holms, gales and storms made life hard and leave unreliable. By 1882 a more efficient force was established. Brean Down and Steep Holm were manned by the 7th Division of the Western District based in Plymouth. The corps offered a free uniform to a certain number of volunteers on condition that they signed on for 3 years. A flood of 50 volunteers appeared at once and 30 were selected.

These ports by 1881 were becoming very busy with an annual number of boats visiting the Channel ports of 39,971, a tonnage of 12,142,791 tons. They were vulnerable to attack, in 1797 a French raiding force was spotted off Lundy and forced by bad weather to dock at Fishguard, but that was intent on destroying Bristol. Even the Americans in the American Civil War boasted that in a war with England they could destroy Cardiff and steal the coal from there and other docks.

With the advent of more sophisticated naval vessels, there was pressure to give greater protection to the Channel ports. By 1891 Torpedo boats were capable of attacking at speeds of 21 knots, and the defenceless state of the Channel caused grave concern. Eventually a gunboat was stationed in the Channel, but more and more local pressure called for a harbour to be built at the end of Brean Down to afford permanent protection.

The site of the fort was well placed on a projecting point of the Down overlooking the sea and, in case of invasion, the hill overlooking the fort could be manned as a defence post.

The fort was enclosed with a high wall, in places part of the barrack structure, and there was a dry moat 12 ft deep and 33 ft wide. A narrow bridge over the moat led to the entrance via an iron gate. Above the main door was a carved stone, VR, and the date of construction. The barracks to the left could accommodate

50 men. (During the 1939–45 war, many additional buildings were constructed). From an inspection of 1882 the following armament was listed.

7–7-inch RML guns, 4 on 'A' pivots. 3 on 'C' pivots.
West facing –2 guns on 'C' pivots. One on 'A' pivot.
NW facing – 3 guns on 'A' pivot.
NE facing – 1 gun on 'C' pivot. Nearby a large underground magazine 18 ft. by 15 ft. and 30 ft. high.
During 1901 all the original guns were sold for scrap.

THE BREAN DOWN DISASTER

The Weston Mercury of 4th of July 1900 carried the heading, 'Magazine Explosion at Brean Down'. At 5.00 am on the 4th of July an explosion destroyed a considerable part of the fort and barracks, killing one soldier and injuring another. Major James Withers who was in charge of the garrison tried to telephone Weston for help but the explosion had destroyed the telephone lines and the messenger had to go by bike. The soldier killed was Gunner Haines from Bridgwater who had only been on the Down for a week, having been posted from Steep Holm. Another soldier, Gunner Reed, was asleep in the Barracks. There was a tremendous rumbling noise and explosion, and his arm was cut by flying glass. There was almost 3 tons of powder in the magazine and it was amazing that the other magazines were not caught up by the explosion. Gunner Kehoe reported that his carbine was missing from the rack at the head of his bed. The enquiry was held at what is now the Berrow Inn, and the inquest found that the explosion was caused by Gunner Haines, 'firing a carbine loaded with ball cartridge down the shaft of the ventilator, whilst in a state of temporary insanity.'

Gunner Haines had been drinking in Burnham and had walked to Brean. It remains a mystery as to why a soldier of 13 years service should be found naked in the magazine armed with a carbine.

The Mercury reporter, though barred from entry to the fort, was able, by climbing to a hilltop overlooking the inside of the fort, to see that the area was covered with wreckage, huge stones were thrown 200 yards. Iron girders were twisted and scattered, and much of the wall demolished.

Gun Drills – As the forts never carried a full complement of gunners, the men had to double up and fire one piece at a time. The gun numbers were continually changed so that each gunner was experienced in different positions in the drills. Firing seawards was important battery practice, and black powder continued to be used until the 1900's because there was a large stock. There was a special allowance of rounds for station practice, and heavy guns fired 3 rounds every other year. During 1889 an additional 6 rounds was given for the 6-inch guns. Firing practice was crude. The target was an anchored barrel and, for night firing, a bull's eye lantern was used. In 1886 'Hong Kong targets' came in; these were towed behind a launch on a long rope.

Uniforms underwent many changes. The caps of 'other ranks' were 3 inches high, black with yellow braid and a yellow button. Staff Sergents had a 1.25 gold wire lace band and 1-inch for sergeants. The forage cap came in in 1883. Officers wore a dark blue cloth cloak with sleeves and a detached cape. NCO's and other men, dark blue greatcoats. Tunics were dark blue cloth with scarlet collar and embroidered grenades changed in 1880 to brass.

Wellington boots were worn and ankle boots were also issued, and, when in marching order, gaiters were worn. The service dress in khaki was not adopted until 1902.

Little evidence is given of communication system between the islands and the mainland, or along Brean Down. The semaphore telegraph system was in use and signal rockets could be used. A telephone is mentioned on Brean Down at the time of the explosion, though it was put out of action.

BREAN DOWN HARBOUR SCHEME

It was in the 1860's that first thoughts of a harbour at Brean Down were mooted. It was thought that with a breakwater at the end of the Down, with the deep channel of the Axe and the shelter afforded by the Down, that a port could be constructed. Ocean ships were smaller than today with shallower draught. There was great industrial expansion in Great Britain and the proximity of the South Wales coalfields made trading from Brean an exciting prospect. Cattle and livestock were imported from lreland, coal came from Wales and rich agricultural produce could be exported from the South Western Counties.

The Post Office too were interested in this as a packet station for the West India Mails, and strong evidence for this was given by two Elder Brethren of Trinity House. Brean Down Harbour was recommended by Admiral Evans, who had been employed in the Post Office Enquiry Commission to examine the Harbours from which the Mails go, and, in his opinion, 'To take England, lreland and Scotland together, there is no part of the Kingdom, in my opinion, so well suited for a Packet Station as Brean Down in the Bristol Channel.'

Costs were put at £350,000, and in 1861 the Brean Down Harbour Company was launched. The proposals included a breakwater, docks and a railway running the length of the Down to link up with the GWR at Lympsham.

To further the plans for the new Harbour, in 1862 the tip of Brean Down was purchased from the William Wyndham Estate for £350. Trinity House backed the scheme, giving evidence before the Select Committee for the advantages of Brean Down as a harbour over any other site in the Channel.

The laying of the Foundation Stone was Saturday, November 5th 1864, and the paddle steamer 'Wye' left Weston with 200 passengers, local dignitaries, the Company's directors and the Town Band.

The band played, volunteers fired a salute, people cheered as Lady Wilmot made a speech as the stone was craned and pulleyed into the air, then lowered into the sea. Lady Wilmot, the wife of

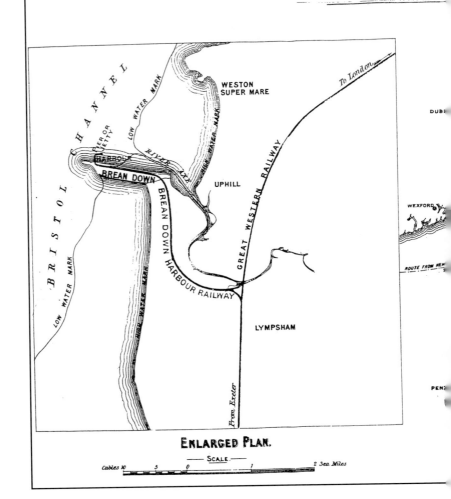

ENLARGED PLAN.

SCALE.

Cables 10   5   0   1   2 Sea Miles

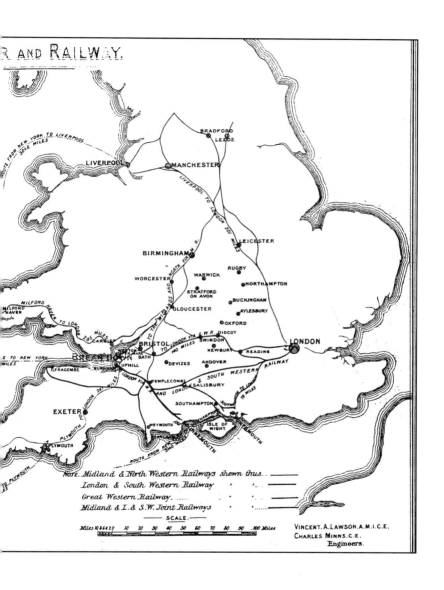

R AND RAILWAY.

VINCENT. A. LAWSON. A.M.I.C.E,
CHARLES MINNS. C.E.
Engineers.

the Chairman of the Company Sir John Eardley Wilmot, extolled the virtues of the new deep water harbour which would be protected by the artillery of Brean Down Fort, then under construction, making a rich trading centre as well as an effective Severn defence.

By next morning the stone had vanished! It had been attached to a buoy with a flag attached with B D H (Brean Down Harbour) on it, and it floated away with the 2½ × 1 ft stone and was found off Steep Holm.

Work did start, however, but severe winter storms, disagreements among personalities, and finally the death of the contractor, Mr Chaplin, in a fatal accident led to the abandonment of the plan.

REVIVAL OF THE 1861 BREAN DOWN HARBOUR PROJECT 1887

Renewed interest in the Harbour Scheme and Railway received much support in Weston-super-Mare, and at a public meeting in 1889, a crowded meeting was hold in the Assembly Rooms under the Presidency of Sir John Eardly Wilmot. He reported that he had been in correspondence with the New York Press who had published an article, 'Five Days to England' – 'The intention is to construct a new harbour, which will still further reduce the distance between England and the United States. The new port is only a few miles from Bristol and 140 miles from London'

The following document was produced to promote the importance of the scheme, and an engineer was appointed to carry out the work. The engineer, Mr Vincent Lawson, told the meeting that the railway along the Down would not only join the main line at Lympsham, but a separate rail line could run direct into Weston Station and the GWR had offered full support.

Revival of the late Brean Down Harbour Project of 1861.
PROPOSED BRISTOL CHANNEL DOCKS CO.,
To be incorporated by Special Act of Parliament.

REPORT ON THE GENERAL FEATURES OF THE PROJECT, AND DRAFT FORM FOR PROSPECTUS.

This Company will be incorporated by Special Act of Parliament for the construction of a Deep-sea Harbour and Docks, accessible to the largest vessels afloat at all states of the tide. The site of the proposed Works is at Brean Down, a lofty promonitory running about a mile and three quarters into the Bristol Channel, about two miles South of the rapidly-growing Town of Weston-super-Mare and nineteen miles from the City of Bristol, its whole Northerly side being well sheltered from the South-westerly winds which prevail in that district during the greater part of the year. The scheme is a revival of the Company and project of 1861, but on a much larger scale, the previous scheme having received a fatal check by the unfortunate death of the contractor, Mr Chaplin, after the foundation-stone had been laid with great ceremony and the works were actively in operation, an Act of Parliament for the construction of a Harbour and Docks at Brean Down and railway connections with the Bristol and Exeter line (now the property of the Great Western Railway Company) having been obtained without opposition.

A Syndicate is now in course of formation to provide the funds for preliminary expenses in preparing the plans necessary for obtaining the requisite Act of Parliament, when the Capital of the proposed new Company will be determined. (which is approximated at £1,500,000.)

ADVANTAGES OF THESE DOCKS

1. The proposed New harbour and Docks would be the most centrally situated, the nearest and most direct Port in the Bristol Channel and West of England for London, the Midland, Western, and Southern Counties trading with North and South America, the West Indies, West Africa, & c. Several eminent authorities on Docks and Harbours have testified as to the great advantages and splendid situation of Brean Down for a Deep-

sea harbour and Docks, and there is no doubt that its position is by far the best in the Bristol Channel and one of the finest in the United Kingdom, both commercially and strategically. And it may be mentioned that Sir John Eardley Wilmot, Bart., (the original promoter of the late Brean Down Harbour Co. of 1861), and other influential gentlemen connected with that project, are cordial supporters of the present undertaking.

2. The saving of time between America and London, as well as to other parts of England, would be one whole day as compared between America and Liverpool. The route for vessels being in a direct line to New York, South of Ireland, and touching or not at Waterford as might be required, thus avoiding the circuitous and sometimes dangerous route by the Irish Channel.

3. Brean Down occupies the finest situation in the country for a Transatlantic Port.

3a. No spot in England is more admirably adapted than Brean Down for telegraphic communication with the United States.

4. As in the present days of keen competition any saving of time is of the utmost importance, it is confidently anticipated that the Government would readily avail themselves of this Port for the despatch of the Mails to America, whilst the same saving of time would be of equal advantage to all other forms of traffic. And in view of the late scheme being carried out, a Company was actually formed in New York for the purpose of establishing a powerful line of Steamships to run to Brean Down as soon as the Harbour was completed. It is anticipated that in addition to the facilities thus afforded for Passenger traffic between the South and West of England and South Wales, a very large Steam Coal Traffic will find its way from the Welsh Coal Fields (Cardiff being nearly opposite Brean Down), via Brean Down Harbour to our Dockyards and Arsenals, as well as to our Commercial Ports on the Bristol Channel. In return, the rich agricultural produce of Wilts, Somerset and Dorset, will supply the thickly-populated mining but non-agricultural districts on the opposite Coast. In addition to this, Brean Down Harbour will furnish an excellent landing place for cattle and other live stock from the South of Ireland, to be transmitted by the shortest and readiest route to the Metropolitan Markets, at the present time the tidal difficulties of the Bristol Channel materially interfering with the safety and regularity of the Irish Trade. But above all, it is confidently expected that lying as Brean Down Harbour

will do, in a straight line between London and New York, and clear of the Southern Coast of Ireland, it must very soon become one of the most important points of departure from this country to America and our North American Colonies.

5. The Docks would be magnificently situated for emigration purposes.

6. There will be no difficulty as regards coaling, and the Aberdare coal, which is some of the best in the country for Steamship purposes, can be supplied direct.

7. The largest vessels afloat could enter the harbour at any time or tide, and no pilot would be required, 'a distinct advantage and saving of time over any other Port in the Bristol Channel,' whilst they would be far easier of access.

8. There is also the great advantage of having abundant supplies of stone for the construction of the Works, which can be obtained on the spot, thus adding, from an economical point of view, an additional merit to the scheme. Workmen can be amply accommodated at Brean Down or Uphill adjoining the site of the proposed Docks, and at the town of Weston-super-Mare.

9. There will be direct connection with the Great Western and Midland Main lines, thus affording direct railway communication between the Harbour and Docks to London, Bristol, Plymouth, Portsmouth, Portland, Southampton and all parts of England, thus enabling them to compete very favourably with any other Docks in the Bristol Channel, whilst less than half of the traffic already done at Cardiff would be sufficient to pay a dividend of 5 per cent. to the Shareholders.

10. There is little need for statistics of traffic to prove that this will be a most successful financial undertaking. The shipping trade of the Bristol Channel has grown to an enormous extent, and is not at least one-fifth of that of the whole of England. Cardiff, situated in this Channel, has gradually become the third largest Port in the Kingdom, and its Dock accommodation is still being largely increased, and the magnificent success of the Bute Docks (now the property of a Company) and their rapidly increasing trade, is sufficient to show that there is every prospect of the Shipping trade in the Bristol Channel continuing to improve.

11. The annual traffic to and from the Midland district, embracing imports and exports, is estimated at about 5,000,000 tons, nearly all of

which at present is carried by the railways communicating with Liverpool, Hull and London, and a number of manufacturers and merchants connected with the commerce of the district stretching from the Midlands to the Bristol Channel have combined to formulate a scheme for placing the Midland Counties in direct communication with the sea by widening the existing waterway between Birmingham and the Bristol Channel. The enormous gain to exporters and importers may be gathered by comparing the present rates with those which would prevail if this plan were in operation. The present rate for hardware from Birmingham to London, Liverpool and Hull averages about 23/- per ton; by the improved waterway the total cost of carriage to the ports in the Bristol Channel would be a maximum and inclusive charge of 14/- per ton. From Liverpool to Birmingham the existing rates for grain and timber are 13/10 and 15/- per ton respectively; by the improved canal the corresponding rates would be about 6/- per ton to the Bristol Channel ports. Of the 5,000,000 tons annually carried to and from the Midlands, about 75 per cent. goes by rail between Hull, Liverpool and London, and only 25 per cent. to the ports in the Bristol Channel. The Midland manufacturers who are eagerly seeking an outlet for their wares would be only too glad to avail themselves of such a port as contemplated at Brean Down, which would be the only harbour in the Bristol Channel and between Gloucester and the Lands-end that would be accessible for vessels of all tonnage at any time of the tide. The Potteries alone import several millions of tons of heavy material which is now driven round by the Mersey route for the lack of better and cheaper communication between the Bristol Channel and the Midlands. And of the £5,000,000 worth of traffic which now goes by railway from the Midlands to other ports, it will be shown that the proposed new docks could almost hope to be supported from the Midland district alone, while it will also be seen that Brean Down is equally well situated for the reception of traffic from all other parts of the country, having complete communication with the Great Western and Midland main lines. The Docks at Brean Down would also benefit the export trade of coal, iron, &c., on the Welsh side of the Bristol Channel, as vessels trading with the Midlands and other parts of England will also have return freights available from Cardiff, Newport, and the other Docks situated on that side of the Channel.

    12. The land at Brean Down belongs entirely to one proprietor, who

is strongly in favour of the scheme and will support it, and most favourable arrangements can be made for the acquisition of the land and property required for the construction of the Works. The land at present is comparatively useless and of little value, and some fine sites for Quays and building accommodation may be obtained at trifling cost. The site of the proposed Docks is quite close to the Great Western main line, and only a short branch line will be required to connect the Docks with that system.

13. The principal imports to the Bristol Channel Ports may be mentioned, as follows:- sugar, rum, molasses, wine, brandy, timber, deals, sleepers, tallow, hemp, turpentine, dye stuffs, palm oil, fruits, grain, seed, oil cake, marble, bones, guano, ores, clay and tea; *and the exports*, coal salt, pitch, iron manufactures, bricks, earthenware, &c., whilst these Ports may also be classed as the great centre of the leather, timber, sugar and wool trades, and the Irish provision trade, having a considerable connection with the West Indies and West Africa.

14. This project, if carried out, will supply a requirement up to the present time very much felt in the Bristol Channel for a deep Sea Harbour accessible to vessels at all states of the tide. No such anchorage now exists, and hence shipwrecks and disasters at sea frequently occur in that locality from a want of a Harbour of Refuge, while passenger and trading communication between the English and the Welsh Ports on either side of the Severn is necessarily interrupted and uncertain.

15. The Severn defences, constructed by Her Majesty's Government, commence on Brean Down, close to the proposed Harbour, and afford it ample protection; these are continued across the Channel by means of powerful batteries on the Islands of Steep and Flat Holmes, terminating at Lavernock Point on the Welsh shore, thus also giving peculiar and great stratagetical advantages.

Extract referring to this project from *Morning Post* dated 6th June 1887

16. Sir John Goode, C.E., and Admiral Evans (the latter employed some years ago to make a Survey of the Bristol Channel), reported that no more eligible site could be found throughout the entire district for the construction of a Harbour of large dimensions, and also that its position as regards the open sea gave it peculiar advantages for a Trans-Atlantic Station, the course of a vessel thence being in a straight line to New York.

BREAN DOWN, the site of the proposed New Docks and Harbour, is also admirably situated for a Harbour of Refuge, and since the heavy loss of vessels and life during the recent great gales (upwards of 50 vessels and 300 lives), a Harbour of Refuge in the Bristol Channel has become an acknowledged and pressing necessity, and a Committee of Inquiry has been appointed for the purposes of inquiring into and selecting a convenient site for some such work. At present Lundy Island seems to find favour as the most suitable site, but the latter would not be of much service to craft further up the Channel, and of course would serve principally for vessels homeward-bound and about entering the Channel, whilst the construction of a Harbour at Lundy Island would be far more costly than at Brean Down. It is of the utmost importance also to have such a Harbour of Refuge that would be as centrally situated as possible, and serve for shelter for the smaller vessels of the local Channel traffic, such as small boats, fishing smacks, coasting boats, &c., as well As for deep-sea-going vessels. The above proposed Harbour will serve most effectually for sheltering the local, channel, and other large shipping traffic in rough weather and at all times of the tide, and the site has been approved of by many eminent maritime authorities both as a deep sea steam-packet Harbour and as a Harbour of Refuge; and it is confidently anticipated that the project will receive the support of the Government, favorable opinions having already been expressed by the Admiralty.

On the opposite page will be found extracts from the Report of Sir John Coode, the eminent Marine Engineer, who examined the site of the proposed Harbour and Docks in 1861.

V A LAWSON, AMICE
Russell Street, STROUD, Glos.

To finance the grand schemes share application forms were produced in order that capital could be raised to finance the plans. Brean Harbour and Railway Act passed through Parliament and received Royal Assent, and were authorised to raise £345,000 by share issue.

This Form of Application should be forwarded in its entirety, accompanied by a Cheque for the Amount of the Deposit on Shares applied for.

THE HARBOUR CONSTRUCTION COMPANY, Limited.

Capital £6,000, in 600 Shares of £10 each.

FORM OF APPLICATION FOR SHARES.

To the Directors of
THE HARBOUR CONSTRUCTION COMPANY, Limited.

GENTLEMEN,

I beg to enclose my cheque for £_____(being a deposit of £2 per Share on Application), and I request you to allot me_____Shares in the above Company, upon the terms of your Prospectus of the 25th day of February, 1889, and of the Memorandum and Articles of Association, and I hereby agree to accept such Shares, or any less number allotted to me, and I authorize you to place my name on the Register of Shareholders, in respect of such Shares allotted to me.

Name (in full) _____

*Address*_____

*Description*_____

*Date*____ _____., 1889.

THE HARBOUR CONSTRUCTION COMPANY, Limited.

RECEIPT FOR DEPOSIT ON APPLICATION FOR SHARES.

(To be Returned to the Applicant.)

*No.*_____

Received *the* _____ *day of*_____ 1889,

on account of THE HARBOUR CONSTRUCTION COMPANY, LIMITED, *from* _____

_____ *the sum of.* _____*Pounds, being a deposit of £2 per*

*Share upon Application for*_____ ____*Shares of £10 each of the above-named Company.*

_____

£ : :

This Receipt should be preserved to exchange for the Share Certificate when the Shares are fully paid up.

COLLAPSE OF THE BREAN DOWN HARBOUR & RAILWAY PROJECT

Despite local enthusiasm for the Harbour scheme, money was not readily forthcoming, and the Railway companies, despite initial enthusiasm, did not cooperate to further the plans. The GWR in Wales cast doubts as to the fact that its monopoly might be jeopardised by the establishment of a ferry service from Wales to Brean Down and its connection at Lympsham to the South Western system. Because the two companies had an agreement that each pledged not to interfere in districts monopolised by the other, the South Western were therefore barred from having any further negotiations with the Brean Down Scheme.

There was some hope that Parliament might intercede to save the scheme, but the main exponents were now growing old and their dreams dying with them, and this bold venture had nothing left to show other than artists' impressions of the planned harbour.

Nothing is known of the £365,000 raised by the sale of shares – it would appear that all contributors lost their money.

EDUCATION IN BREAN

Prior to the opening of the village school, illiteracy in the village was high. Even the ability to write their own name was beyond the capabilities of many in Brean, particularly among the women whose parents did not believe it was necessary to educate girls whose job was to marry, have children and work in the home and the farm.

Those children who did learn to read and write were from the wealthier families who attended 'Dames Schools' – small private schools which ladies in towns and villages set up, charging a few pence per week. Usually the teachers were not qualified in any way and the schools not inspected. Wealthier homes employed private governesses and, until Breane Village School opened in 1874, the percentage of Literate Brides (i.e. able to sign their name) was very low but rose dramatically after the School opened. This was one of the last villages to have a school, since in 1811 the National Society of the Church of England aimed to provide a Church School in every parish, but it was 1880 before attendance at school became compulsory.

The first teacher appointed to the National School at Breane was Miss Rowles at a salary of £40 per year, with a schoolhouse provided. The School Committee was Rev TW Strong, Messrs

Rev T Strong, Chairman of the School
Governors

47

J Cox (Diamond Farm), T H Curry (Manor Farm), P Harris (Warren Farm).

The Church societies guarded their rights to schools in their care jealously and were opposed to state interference, but usually had to accept joint control in order to get state financial aid. Breane National School received its first grant aid in 1897, and in 1904, had Church members, parish members and representatives of the County Education Committee, on its governing board. Miss Rowles only stayed one year and was succeeded by Miss Marriott, who, again, only lasted a year. They found themselves in a remote rural community, the only teacher in a school, not accepted by the farmers as the 'upper class', nor members of the labouring class and their families.

In 1882 Reverend Thomas Strong arrived as Rector of Breane. He had a degree, MA from Oriel College, Oxford, and believed strongly in education. Not only was he largely responsible for the restoration of the Church, but he was a very strong supporter of the Village School, Chairman of the Governors, visited at least once a week, inspected and signed the attendance register.

The next headmistress to be appointed was Emma Comfort Ashworth. She was born in 1864, and was a pupil teacher at a school in Brighton from 1882–85, when she left to train as a teacher. Her qualifications obtained in 1886 and 1887 seem today to be very strange subjects to fit her to be headmistress of a village school:–

Certificate in Principles of Agriculture 1886. Advanced.
Magnetism & Electricity 1887.
Drawing.

She was appointed at a salary of £60.00 per year and had two part-time Monitresses, Lucy Millier (who lived in the thatched cottage at Brean Down) and Lilian Palmer. One did mornings and one afternoons, and they did housework the other half of the day.

The first Log Book of the school in the Somerset County Records is of 1912, and no details of the school seem to be recorded before this. Eighteen children were present as being in attendance, and this was very good, frequently 100%. being present. The Log Book goes into considerable detail of the Health of the children, absenteeism is accompanied by details of illnesses causing absence. In such a small school infectious diseases spread rapidly and, as there were several members of families all at the school at the same time, they tended to all catch the same infection.

There were frequent Medical Inspections. On July 17th 1912 the Medical Inspector attended, the parents of Stanley Harris and Ralph Harris refused to send them to school on the day of the Medical examination, so they were excluded from school until they had been examined.

Measles seems to have been very prevalent and, when rife, caused a big drop in attendance. Measles had to be reported to the Sanitary Inspector. In 1914 the school had to be closed July 8th–27th, there were so many cases of measles. Influenza caused a number of absences, but one of the worst outbreaks of infection was that of Ringworm. Some children had body ringworm, some had face infections, but the worst outbreak was of head ringworm. This was probably caused by milking cows with the head pressed against the cow's body. A number of children were excluded and only allowed back with their heads shaven, and wearing a medical cap. Fred Davis is shown in the school picture wearing a hat which he refused to take off till his hair grew.

Whooping Cough set children back badly. In April 1923 Harry Hobbs was away for 11 weeks with whooping cough and Victor Hobbs for 8 weeks. There was one case of TB recorded, and one boy who had to be watched carefully as he had epileptic fits.

The school was frequently visited by Nurse Toms, as well as the Medical Examiner, and children were taken to Brent Knoll to the County School Dentist. On June 28th 1923 seven scholars were taken to have their teeth withdrawn.

Other absences were caused by weather, 'attendance not so good due to a fearful whirling wind and rain'. In Summer the boys were frequently withdrawn to help with haymaking, and the boys often left school at 12–13 needed to help on the farm, when they had to have special exemption certificates. Ralph Harris, Willie Flynn and Arthur Harris had a day off school on June 30th

1920 to take part in a County Council Milking Competition at Huntspill.

Despite these absences in the early years of the school, attendance was very good and frequently remarked upon by the Inspectors. The Diocesan Inspection of 1912 says:–

> 'Mixed & Infant – The classes at this little country school is unusually good considering the distance they have to travel.
> The Mistress manages very well considering the different grades she has to teach together, with fair success.
> Reading fairly well. Mental arithmetic – very creditable. Remember little poetry. Recitation monotonous and not understood.
> The repetition of the Catechism of the Upper Group showed evidence of patient and continuous teaching. Most of the girls and one or two of the boys answered nicely.
> The babies need individual attention. Bible story pictures should be used.
> The Lords Prayer should be taught. The syllabus should be enlarged. The tone of the school is good'.

As this was a Church School it was inspected by the Diocese for religious teaching and the County Council for general education.

> September 12th 1912. Inspected by HMI Mr Stacey.
> July 14th 1912. County Inspector of Drill. Miss McDougall.
> June 13th 1913. There was a visit from the Sewing Inspectress (Miss Robinson).

However, on the whole, attendance in the early days was very good and Rev T Strong, as Chairman of Governors, not only visited the school frequently and signed the register, but also gave out attendance prizes. The Log Book frequently notes, 'Attendance Perfect'. In 1912 Rev T Strong awarded medals and books to 6 children who had made perfect attendances, and books to 4 others who had attended 400 times in the year. (A day's attendance counted as 2, morning and afternoon).

Good behaviour and regular schooling was rewarded by school treats, an afternoon off and time spent at the rectory and in the garden, at Christmas Rev. Strong gave the school a Xmas tree and there was a school trip to Burnham to the Puzzle Gardens. (Later this became a pub called the 'Puzzle Garden' and had a maze in the front.) The children travelled in a wagonette with their teacher, Miss Ashworth. It was her last day at school and she left to go to Lancashire at £100 per year. The school syllabus spent a lot of time on aspects of the 3 R's, but was criticised by inspectors as not showing much opportunity for original thought and composition. Much learning was by rote and recitation by the whole class, so that the poorer children were hidden by the better. But one teacher had to cover a wide age range and ability level, so there was little time for individual attention.

Exam subjects were:–

Class I	Class II
Reading	Writing
Dictation	Reading
Composition	Arithmetic
Grammar	Drawing
Geography	Tables
History	Dictation
Arithmetic	
Drawing	
Tables	

Exam results in 1914 show a mixed set of figures:-

E Kerton 66%	K Kerton 85%	S Coles 64%
J Coles 66%	E Greenham 57%	C Kerton 54%
W Greenham 37%	F Kerton 47%	E Coles 65%
B Davis 46%	E Kerton 64%	S Flynn 34%
C Greenham 63%	L Greenham 28%	

There is nothing to show the children's ages, but as 3, 4, 5 children have the same name, there must have been a wide age range between brothers, sisters, cousins. In February 1914 disaster struck the school when the Headmistress, Mrs Hardwick, died suddenly. There followed a period of disruption. In July, Maud Brown was appointed but resigned in October. In December, Jane Garland was appointed. She resigned shortly after and, in fact, in 2 years the school had 4 Head Teachers. Finally Mrs Roberts was appointed and was Head for more than 16 years. It is scarcely surprising that Head teachers did not remain. £60 a year was not much reward for a hard day's work as the sole teacher. Though various monitresses were appointed, they were usually in charge of the infants, and their training consisted of a week at Brent Knoll.

They too had their trials. One lady, still alive today, describes how she was sent to school aged 3½ years because her Mother was having another baby and was too busy to cope. The first day, missing her home, father and mother, she cried all morning, till the teacher could stand it no longer, took her out of class and sat her on her own in a corner out of the way. So frightened was the infant that she wet her knickers and was sent home! This was just what the child wanted, so the next day the performance was repeated! But Mother was sharper than this small girl, and each day she was sent with spare knickers and soon learnt that it was preferable to sit and endure the school day than to be on the cold stone floor and be changed. She later learnt to love the little school.

It is little wonder that teachers did not last long, and surprising that Mrs Roberts lasted 16 years. Both the buildings, facilities and discipline gradually declined. Little money was spent on maintenance and repairs, and materials needed by the children were old and worn.

Very little money was spent on books and equipment – records show in 1902:–

Books and stationery £3.12.6.
Apparatus and furniture £1.15.0.

Fuel, lighting, cleaning £2.12.1
Repairs £2.11.0
Rent £4.10.5.
Teacher's lodgings (part of her emoluments) £5.00
Tax £9.7.0.
Needlework £2.7.7.
Total £97.18.2. Grant Aid £8.00

Each school had to make returns showing their buildings.

1903 Returns
How many rooms used for instruction – 2
Size main room 24 × 13.3
Side room 10 × 13.3
Cloakrooms 6 × 10 & 4 × 9½ – 2
Gym apparatus None.
How far away are closets and urinals – 21 yards.
Are they separate each sex – yes.
What is maximum accommodation of the school – 46.
Present total numbers   *Boys*   Girls
                       15   16   Total 31.
Is the building used for other purposes.
Parish meetings. Entertainments and lectures.
Maintenance £95.17.6.
Grants Bd. Of Education £73.70 Deficit £22.10.6
Endowment – No.
School fees – None.

The premises were in a poor state of repair. The entrance to the girls' toilets were blocked with sand and stinging nettles. The playground needed fencing and the surface was potted with holes and frequently flooded. School heating was poor and often very cold in winter.

In 1912 the only books bought were 1 dozen poetry books and the request for two thermometers took months to be implemented. The infants' books were all over 5 years old, and in 1914 it was reported that part of the class had to write in pencil because the

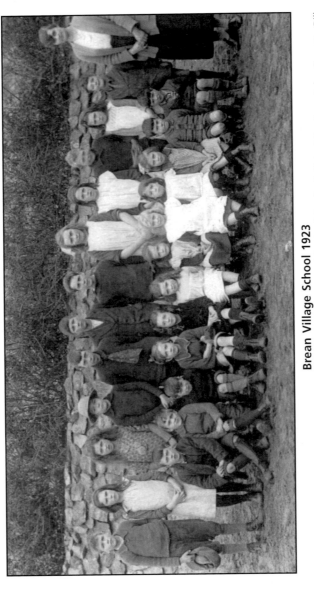

Brean Village School 1923

Back row – left to right: Tom Hardiman, May Kerton, Irene Puddy, Fred Davis, Jeff Leddington, John Perrett, Bill Kerton, Ann Durston, Kathleen Flynn, Roy Leddington, ?, Student teacher – Blanche Davis.

Front row: Henry Puddy, Nelson Durston, Bert Puddy, Gladys Perrett, Kathleen Harris, Dora Durston, Evelyn Davis, Grace Hooper, Lily Flynn, Bessie Hobbs, Victor Hobbs, ?.

pens were so bad and the pencils not fit for drawing. The arithmetic was hindered because there were no suitable textbooks

Educational standards were poor, but the teachers received no formal teacher training and assistance was from older pupils who stayed on after the age of 13. Blanche Davis (shown in the school photograph), finished school on June 25th and received her exemption certificate, August 9th she started as a monitress, aged 13. In 1914 the girls were recorded as having done extra needlework in order to finish two garments donated to Belgian refugees.

The children all appeared to be able to read and write and do simple arithmetic when they left school, but few, if any, went on to any further education. The boys mostly joined their fathers doing farm work and the girls going into service. Lessons do not seem to have been inspiring. The log book lists one day's 'Object Lesson' as 'The Periwinkle'.

The school premises, when they were first used as a school, were described as 'cottage premises in Church Rd. Brean'. In 1895 they were altered and enlarged to make the 2 rooms which were described in the returns of 1903, a second room having been built on with a sliding door in between so that it could be turned into one big room. During all this time it was rented from Mr Henry Adams Hicks at a rent of £4.00 a year. But in 1903 it came on the Market for Sale. Mr TO Wethered was a wealthy brewer who came each summer to 'The Manor' at Brean, moving in with a retinue of servants. He purchased this property and, in 1909, presented the parishioners of Brean with their village school, to be administered by nine local men as trustees.

Mrs Roberts, the Headmistress appointed in 1917, inherited a difficult school. There had been four head teachers in 2 years and discipline and behaviour in the village school was deteriorating.

Mrs Roberts was not content to settle into the village and moved into the Commercial Hotel in Burnham. She was not prepared to be under the watchful eyes of the village, or have her free time observed by the Rector. Wagging tongues said she was not averse to the charms of the Commercial's beer, wines and spirits, and scandalised many Brean inhabitants by arriving in school driven by the proprietor in a motor bike and side car.

Sally Kerton.

The first reports of bad behaviour were made. Children who brought their lunch to school behaved badly in the dinner break, running around without their hats and coats. In winter they interfered with the stove which they were not allowed to touch. Evelyn Davis and Grace Hooper were caned on their hands for being rude and impertinent.

One set of parents complained that the school was dirty and unhealthy and kept their two boys away from school. Educational standards declined, and Inspectors' reports spoke of the low standard of answers given and in 1926 the County Education Committee transferred all children over 11 to Brent Knoll School.

Mrs Roberts' health was declining. She was becoming very deaf and, after lunch, would nod off at her desk. It was then that the events of the often told story took place. Evelyn Davis, the tallest girl in the school, sat in the back row underneath the school clock. 'Put it on Davy', the boys would mutter and she'd reach up and change the hands of the clock and they'd wake Mrs Roberts with, 'It's time for the bus Miss' – and school would end early!

On the way home from school the children used to call in on Sally Kerton. She lived in a one up and one down house next to the present chapel. Sally always wore a big white apron and was the maid at the Rectory. The children always went in and asked for a drink, because Sally had a well in the garden, and they loved to pull up a bucket of water and drink from it.

Mrs Roberts resigned in 1933 and Somerset decided to close the school. Both educationally and financially the Education Authorities decided on this measure faced with the difficulty of getting a suitable Head. The children were then driven each day to Brent Knoll School.

PRIVATE SCHOOLS

During this time two other schools had opened in Brean. The first was called Brean House School and was in the two houses outside the old entrance to Northam Farm in South Road.

The house at the Burnham end now called 'Merrywood Cottage', and the second, St. Michael's, was built as the school house. This had a large assembly room and school room downstairs and two other rooms upstairs. The toilet was across the yard at the end of what had been the stable and coach house. (When sewerage first came to Brean and main drainage was laid it was found that the old pipe ran across the road and into the land opposite, now the foot of 'Tideways').

The Headmistress was Mrs Manning, a redoubtable lady who used to have a cold bath every morning, summer and winter, before starting school. Every evening she used to have her supper with Mrs Davis.

Stuart Hicks was sent to this school, aged 5, and his mother sat on the bank on the opposite side of the road all the first day in case he was homesick. Between the dunes on this side of the road was a flat sandy patch beside the bridle path, and the children from the school spent their breaks at play there.

57

A second private school was 'Felicia' further down the village in Coast Road. This building was a black hut and girls coming home from Burnham, having been for a Saturday treat at the pictures, could only get a bus to Heron House and had to walk to Brean. They always ran past 'Felicia' because they believed it was haunted.

Brean House School, in the garden of Northam Farm.
Left to rights – standing: Phil Champion, Leslie Harris, Roland Frost, Arthur Frost, Ralph Harris, Guy Manning, Stan Harris, Bruce Harris, John Strong.
Front row – sitting: Arthur Harris, Betty Frost, Vera Champion, Betty Champion, Ken Champion, Hilda Harris, Joan Harris, Freda Harris.

CHEESEMAKING ON BREAN FARMS

Most of the farms in Brean made cheese. Just as nowadays we have 'Scottish' Cheddar, 'Canadian' Cheddar, so the best cheese made in Brean was Caerphilly. Originally cheesemakers from Wales came over to teach the art to Somerset farmers, but soon Brean cheese was being sent to Wales, to Bristol, London and many other cities.

In 1912 milk went to the Milk Factory at Bason Bridge. It was wheeled to the farm gate on a low trolley in churns, and the filled churns collected and empties left at the gate transported in a horse-drawn milk lorry.

Warren Farm delivered milk through most of Brean and into Berrow, though later this end of the round was made by Northam Farm.

Caerphilly cheese was made in Spring and Autumn, though some farms such as Brean Down Farm produced it all the year round. Most of the cheese was taken by horse and cart to Highbridge market, but some went to a repository in Market Street, Highbridge, where it was stored until sent by rail. The cheeses sent by rail were packed in straw and sent to the cities.

The Caerphilly was sold in small rounds called truckles of about 7–8 lbs. 10 inches round and 3 ins. deep and it yielded more weight per gallon of milk than Cheddar. The Cheddar cheeses were bigger, heavier rounds. One of the advantages of Caerphilly was that it could be sold at 2–3 weeks old and did not have to be kept long to mature.

The horse and cart used to take cheese to market also took the pigs to market at Highbridge, covered with a net to stop them jumping out, and then returned filled with coal!

In the 1920's, 9d. a lb. was a good price for cheese, a cheese-maker got 12/6 a week and usually lived at the farm, or in one of the farm cottages. Most of the farms employed cheesemakers; at Northam Miss Knapp was employed, but Vera Champion went away to Cannington Farm Institute and trained to be a cheese-maker, and eventually took her place. At Warren Farm Miss Mullett was the cheesemaker, and their cheeses won many prizes

59

at local shows and big events, such as the Bath & West and London Dairy Show. One of their prize years resulted in their providing the King's Shoot at Sandringham with cheese.

At Northam Farm, when the cheese had been made in the dairy, it was put on a hoist which was wound by hand up through the dairy roof, through a bedroom and into the attic, where it was stored at one end of the large airy room and lovely apples, like Tom Putt and Morgan Sweets, were stored at the other end. It is only in the last few years that this lift has been removed.

The old dairy and outbuildings shown in the photo of Northam have been pulled down now to make room for campers' requirements, though the old farm is still there. Built in C18 the dairy was at the end of the house with the lift up through the bedroom above it. From the dairy led a boiler house and pail shed where pails and churns were scrubbed and stored. An underground pipe led to the pigsties for the whey from the dairy to be run out to the pigs where, mixed with cereal, it was used to fatten the livestock.

Behind the dairy was the wash-house. Mrs Davis came across

Northam Farm – outside the Dairy.
Vera Champion purling the mop. Mrs Champion in doorway.

from her cottage every Monday to boil the washing, and Tuesday was spent doing the ironing. The photo shows Vera Champion purling the mop after cleaning the dairy, water flying from it (no squeezee then), the mop was made of old rags, old trousers and strips of material attached to a wooden handle. Her mother, Mrs Champion is in the doorway behind.

Most farms were mixed dairy and kept cattle, sheep, pigs and hens, as well as growing crops. The women were expected to help on the farm as well as the men and children. Attendance at the village school was very irregular and boys, and sometimes the girls, were frequently absent and helping on the farm, and most left school at 12–13 to help full time.

In the War, Land Girls came to help on the farms. They came from a wide variety of homes and backgrounds and office work, often with no experience of farm life. They had to work very hard and very long hours, usually living with other farm workers in the farm cottages. The Land Army had an 'Army Welfare Officer' who visited the farms once a month to help the girls with any problems they had, and to see that they were fairly treated. Many

Phil & Fred Champion. Bull Nose Morris tractor conversion.

farmers and their wives made the land girls very welcome into their homes socially, and some stayed in touch for many years.

In common with other agricultural workers, land girls got double cheese ration to help with the hard physical labour involved, but since the weekly cheese ration was only 2 oz. per person per week, this probably did not guarantee a great deal more energy!

MEMORIES OF BREAN RESIDENTS
An original contribution to 'Coastline'
MY GRANDMOTHER — EVELYN BAGG

'A Zummerzet Doman, Barn and Bred'. (These were her words). 'Barn out Merlynch way 'tother side o 'Burdgewater. No time for Eddication, I were out under the cows afore I were 9 year old.' Granny didn't go to school, so she couldn't read or write. It puzzled me for a long time why she could sign her name (Mary Ann Davis) with an X, and why Mr Morris, who kept the Brean Post Office, would pay her 10 shillings a week for putting an X on a book. (Of course, I later learnt this was her OLD AGE PENSION!)

I don't ever remember her calling me by my Christian name. I was always 'her maiden'.

She had 15 children, she used to say, 11 Boys and 4 Maidens, and was so proud of them all.

Granny was always working hard. She went milking twice a day, took in washing, and was always ready to help anyone who was ill. Often 'sitting up' at night with someone who was very ill. She also acted as Midwife. She used to say, 'I should have been a NUSS'. She had wonderful remedies for everything. I can remember her taking a leaf from a certain plant, bruising it and tying it round anything that needed healing. She had an endless supply of clean white rag which she bound around everything from grazed knees to cut fingers.

If I had a cold she would say – 'You'm wheezing like an old DUN COW, 'tis goose grease and brown paper for you tonight, maiden', or if I had earache, she would bake an onion in the oven, take out the hot core and 'shove it in yer earhole', and tie it round with a scarf.

In Springtime, it was Brimstone and Treacle, (which I loved), 'you won't get any spots', she would say. She always knew when the seasons began and ended, and never seemed to be a day out either way. One thing I always remember her telling me – 'Button to chin 'till May be in, and cast no clout till May be out.' This was always the month of May. She knew almost to the day when the

'Red Flannel' vests, which my granded wore, had to be taken out of moth balls and thoroughly aired. Granny always wore a cook's white apron fastened at the back with a huge safety pin. Her hair was scraped back into a bun, and when she wore her Sunday Best Black Hat, she speared it to this bun, with two of the most enormous hat pins I had ever seen.

For milking, she always had a clean white coat, a man's cap, and hob-nailed boots. She was such a jolly person with a wonderful sense of humour. I think the only time I ever saw her cross was one morning – she came in from milking covered in mud etc. from head to toe. Because 'Bluebell, the varmint, stuck her voot in me pail, afore I could spank her, she tips me off me stool head over heels (or words to that effect!!) THAT'S the VUST time she ever done that, must have 'ad a VLY round her tail'.

I also believed everything Granny told me, and she used to play tricks on me whenever she could. She once sent me to the Butcher's Cart (he came from Lympsham once a week), to ask the butcher for a sheep's head, but tell 'im to leave the front legs on!! Which, in all innocence I did! I would often sleep at Granny's house, although we only lived next door, and my favourite time was sitting on a little stool in front of a blazing fire having supper, and Granny would cut me a 'Gurt crust of Billy Thorne's Bread, and a hunk of Champion's cheese, with a hot mug of cocoa.'

Grandad would be reading aloud from the 'Christian Herald'. Then, it was 'Come on up wooden hill', Granny going on ahead with a hot flat iron, which she ironed all over the sheets. 'Hop in quick afore it gets cold'. Then, watching through the crack of the bedroom door as the candlelight disappeared down the stairs. 'Goodnight Gran'. 'Goodnight my Maiden'.

THE CAFÉ AT BREAN DOWN FORT — IRENE SAMPSON

After the collapse of the Brean Down Harbour Scheme the land returned to the Wyndham family, and then in the 1920's it was leased from Mr Wyndham by the coal hauliers in Weston, W H Hillman.

The fort was still in a reasonable state of repair at this time and the main block, the soldiers' quarters, were made into a café.

Mr and Mrs Meredith lived in Brean village during the winter, but were employed in summer to run the café. They lived in the converted officers' block, during the season. They were staunch members of the Wesleyan Chapel.

The café opened each year on Good Fridays and was open for the summer months only, but as befitted strict chapel members, closed on Sundays.

In March the café was spring-cleaned each year and Mr Hillman brought out a lorry filled with tinned foods and non-perishable goods to last the summer. Other supplies came in by boat during the summer.

No cooked meals were served at the café, there were no facilities for ambitious menus but a cup of tea for four pence a cup could be served indoors or on benches out of doors. Tea with bread and butter was one shilling, with cakes one shilling and three pence, and with jam, one shilling and sixpence.

Irene Sampson was the waitress. She and her family lived in the cottage next to the old Wesleyan Chapel (now T'ween Cottage) which is now a Beauty Parlour. She had a job which no waitress nowadays would expect to put up with. Every day she cycled to Brean Down, collecting cans of milk from Brean Farm and any mail which had been left for the Merediths and the bread left by Baker Thorne. It was hard work pushing her bike up the hill onto the Down, and then riding along the rough track to the Fort.

Once there she was expected to help lay out the tables, there could be places for one hundred and conditions were primitive. Water came from a well and was then kept in storage tanks, and water was boiled on Valor oil stoves which had to be used for making drinks, washing up and washing table cloths, tea towels etc.

Once a week Irene was sent into Weston to fetch chocolate supplies for the café. She cycled to the ferry, crossed the Axe on the ferry to Uphill, caught the bus into Weston and did the shopping; then made the return journey.

Mr Meredith too did his share of cycling. If bread supplies ran out, he had to cycle into Brean to pick up supplies and, once a week, he cycled into Burnham to the Bank with all the café takings ready to be deposited. This could be quite a heavy load, since visitors were charged 1d each to cross the drawbridge into the fort, as well as the takings of the café.

Large bus parties sometimes booked at the café, coming by bus from as far away as Bristol, and parties from Weston came over by boat and ferry. Irene remembers a party of orphans coming from Bristol. There was a lawn outside the café and swings that children could play on, but these children, though treated to a grand tea, did not seem to know how to play and sat quietly after their meal.

Other girls from Brean found early employment at the Down Café. Evelyn Bagg can remember school holidays when she earned her first pocket money there in 1928, cycling out with two or three other girls, to be there by 12.00 midday and finishing at 6.00 pm after helping with the washing up and serving teas.

The café did not remain open for many years. Weather conditions on the Down making catering a hazardous guessing game, it was very hard work with primitive conditions existing and, certainly today, would hardly pass hygiene requirements. The massive numbers, which Sedgemoor hoped to attract to the Fort café in their 1995 plans, would seem like 'pie in the sky'.

THE LIFE OF A LOCAL RESIDENT IN WARTIME BREAN — EVELYN WORMALD

'My husband enlisted, he hoped to go in the Navy as the sea was his great love, but there was greater need in the Air Force, so that's where he was sent, and was away from me and my two children for four and a half years.

Life was difficult, food was rationed and most of the men were away. I started a vegetable garden and that kept us well supplied.

(I was very excited when digging one day I found a Stone Age Flint and I've kept that).

Every day we were down to the beach to drag up wood. My husband made me a saw bench and every morning I spent some time sawing logs for the fire.

On the beach there were some wooden stakes with chicken wire round them, and every day a man with a box on wheels came along and collected the fish caught in the chicken wire. I used to run down to the beach and he would fill a pail of fish for 1/6d.

Then the old man stopped coming so I started my own fishing. Some I got from the netting, but then I started baiting my own lines with strips of herring. These were put out before the tide came in and then I rushed down as it receded, and before the gulls pinched the fish and collected my catch. Lovely fish were caught – cod, skate, conger, sole and once a salmon.

Black American troops were stationed in Deans Holiday Camp (before Pontins), and they were quite a shock for Brean. Going down to the beach one day, three of them were coming out of a beach hut we had there. I said, What are you doing here', and they replied, 'Sorry Ma'am, we were only having a rest'. They were very nice and well behaved, but it was quite a shock on my own.

British Officers were also billeted in the village and their orderlies were often bored and looking for something to do. They offered to help me and, as we'd never put garden steps in, they built my garden steps up to the front door, so that is why they are all odds and evens, but it was wonderful of them and I always remember them as I walk up.

Then they decided I needed an air raid shelter so proceeded to fill sandbags and put them all on the roof of the garage, which had been built into the sand dune – but had to stop that because the roof was falling in!

A gang of men were on the beach putting concrete posts in, and we had them all up sitting on the grass having cups of tea. Then our rations ran out and they had to have cocoa (that was off ration) and one day we gave them all bread pudding. I started keeping hens in the hut they left behind, and used to swap 2 eggs for a little extra butter. But, when we had to eat one of them, I had to get Mr Phil Champion to come and kill it (I ran away whilst he did the deed, I couldn't bear to watch – but one twist and the deed was done). Then I had to skin the rabbits or dress the chicken. We fed the hens on potato peelings and they wandered on the dunes; that was really free range. My friends at Martins Hill Farm sometimes could spare me a bag of cereals and, after harvest, we used to glean to gather some extra grain.

Champions used to deliver milk in a churn and filled our jug or a bottle, woe betide us if we had a bottle and not return it – everything was so precious then.

We heard the bombers going over to Cardiff and to Bath and Bristol. As we had no shelter, we got under the big oak dining room table when we heard the sirens or if bombs were dropping. We had a mother and two children evacuees, who were very badly behaved, and we all had to go under the table together, but they soon went back to London. Incendiary bombs were dropped near the Church and, after that, I always kept buckets filled with sand because a lot of incendiaries dropped on Brean.

For a rest we went up to stay with my Mother in Surrey. That was a dreadful journey with two small children, into Burnham, on the S & D railway to Evercreech, up to London and down to Surrey. She had an Anderson shelter but, because it was so ugly, had it at the bottom of her garden. Then the raids on London started and we had to run all down the garden to the shelter. After about 10 days we decided it was more peaceful back in Somerset.

Living along the road from us was old Kitch. He lived in a shed-cum chalet and sold stamps and a few assorted sweets which the children loved to buy. However it wasn't long before he was interned, because it was thought he might be a German spy. Great excitement for Brean!

At the end of the war my husband was demobbed, complete with 50 shilling de-mob suit, and there was a grand village party for the families and children organised by Mr Hatherall and others. I remember boiling hams – goodness knows where we managed to get them but it was a grand day!'

After the war Mr and Mrs Wormald took over Brean Post

office where Evelyn started a 'free library' from the vast stock of her own books.

Later they opened a second Post office where Allens is now and had to call it Brean Camp Post office. For 2 years they ran both shops, then sold out to Mr and Mrs Allen & their son Barry.

BREAN IN WARTIME 1939–45

In 1939 Brean Down was re-garrisoned, ex-naval Coastal Guns and Lewis Guns were placed there for defence of the Channel, air defences and a searchlight battery. At Weston, HMS Birnbeck was established by the Admiralty Department of Miscellaneous Weapons Development and many strange devices were tried out here and on Brean Down and surrounding beaches, where devices such as the 'Expendable Noise Maker' were tested. (This was designed to decoy and lure German submarines and acoustic torpedoes away from their targets).

Catapult tracks were laid on Brean Down for testing missiles, 'Hedgehog' rounds were fired from Birnbeck Pier, and the high rise and fall of the tides round Brean and Weston meant that projectiles could be recovered.

'Hedgehog' was a forward firing anti-submarine weapon mounted on a ship which could encircle a submarine with mortar charges. 'Hedgehog' missiles played an important part in the destruction of U-boats. They were responsible for the sinking of U531 and U125 and in 1943 caused the Germans to withdraw from the Atlantic, having lost 41 U-boats. On the German return to the Atlantic later that year, U282 was also sunk by 'Hedgehog' missiles.

One projectile fired from Brean, went well the first time, but the second, fired along the water's edge, turned after a few hundred yards and travelled inland towards a farm. Setting off to look for it, the launch crew met a furious local farmer – 'the bugger landed in me chicken run' and 'where were you?' – 'in the bloody chicken run' – this experiment was moved to a quieter area and, though the story is well known in Brean, may have been embroidered over the years!

At the end of 1942 Dr Barnes Wallis was contacted regarding work he was doing on the 'bouncing bomb'. This was successfully used against the Ruhr dams and a seaborne version was experimented with, launching from motor torpedo boats. A ramp was built on Brean Down and a trolley loaded with rockets launched, which promptly burst into flames, scattered all the surrounding safety emplacements and roared over the cliff edge to vanish in the sea.

Brean had an active Local Defence Volunteer Unit during the war, later called the Home Guard, and an Air Raid Precaution force (the ARP) which had to be surprisingly active. A mock aerodrome was built on the levels by the Axe; it was lit up at night to divert bombers away from Bristol and, because of this, and because many bombers dropped their incendiaries returning from bombing the Channel ports, the ARP were kept busy.

In 1940 a Tiger Moth on a training flight from Weston crashed into the sea off Brean, 2 airmen died and their bodies were brought ashore at low tide.

Pillboxes were built along the coast (some of which still survive in gardens along the dunes and on Berrow golf course), sand-bagged trenches were dug in the dunes covered in corrugated iron with sandbags on top. Slit lookouts provided openings for training fire practice. The Army were billeted in summer bungalows along the dunes and marched from here to other villages.

There were coils of barbed wire on parts of the beach and rows of concrete posts were embedded in the sand to prevent landing craft coming ashore. At the end of the war these were removed but some have remained and become covered or uncovered with sand according to the vagaries of the wind.

Most homes had London evacuees housed on them which was a strange learning period for hosts and visitors. One mother and three children from Plaistow, who had never seen the sea before, were sent down to play on the beach until tea was ready. The tide was as far out as only it can go at Brean. After 10 minutes they returned and, when asked whey they were back so soon, tea was not ready, said, 'we were frightened, I've read about tidal waves and didn't know if one would come'. Members of the American army were at the Holiday Camp, Dean's Camp, where much repair of vehicles was done, and others were on Brean Down. Hugh Harris remembers some of them coming to Warren Farm for a bath (were there none at Dean's Holiday Camp?), and in return, presenting the family with three lorry loads of wooden boxes, strong ammunition boxes with rope handles, which they used for

71

years for feeding the calves, for storage and some for firewood.

THE HOME GUARD

Many local farmers were not called up during the 2nd World War, as they were in Reserved Occupation required to work on the farms. Others were too old to become regulars, or perhaps were not physically fit, but instead they formed the Local Defence Volunteers. Churchill later insisted that these be called the Home Guard. This was hard work for the farmers. They were up in summer at 5.00 am doing hard physical labour all day, not finishing till dusk, then having to clean equipment, sharpen knives, make running repairs on equipment and then go on Home Guard duty 3 nights a week.

Three men per night were on duty at the Home Guard Post, known as 'the Summer House' in the little field of Brean Farm where the Land Yacht Club now has a building, and where there was one large bed. Two men were permitted to sleep and one was supposed to be awake, but, if all was quiet, there would be 'three in a bed'! Stuart Hicks remembers Hugh Palmer was always in the middle and 'when the middle one said TURN OVER they all turned over!' Stuart was the first member of the LDV and still has his card.

WPBB 86/3 Private CoyC.

There were no weapons issued to begin with, most of the farmers had their own shotguns and, other than this, there were pitchforks or drain rods. Later 303 rifles were issued and then withdrawn again, because they 'were too good for the Home Guard' and needed elsewhere. It was nearly a year before uniform was issued and, until then, all they had was an armband.

On Sundays the Home Guard went to Church Parade, but they also went onto Brean Down where the Regular Army was stationed. They all met in the yard of the village school, and then were taken by bus up onto the Down and out to the Fort. The bus

DRIVER: CAN'T YOU SEE WE'RE UMPIRES?
GUARD: I DON'T CARE IF YOU'RE FOUR MATERNITY NURSES —

YOU DON'T PASS!

THE CORPORAL MAKES "CONTACT" WITH THE ENEMY WHILST RECCONOITERING THE BARBED WIRE.

Disbanding of Brean & Berrow Home Guard, 1945.
Among the Home Guard members: Mr Dill, R Talbot, Phil Frost, John
Perrett, David Plimley, G Coggins, Tom Westcott, Mr Foster, Mr Freak,
Ben Harris, Gordon Harris, Bill Tucker, John Lynham, Toby Smith (the
smallest man in the Company wearing his military medal from 1914–18
war.), Frank Boobyer, Phil Champion, Horace Pitty, Mr Chick and 3rd
from right – seated, is Col L M Stevens DSO Commanding 13 Battalion.

was so loaded, and the corner at the top so tight, that they had to
get out and push. John Tucker's father, William Tucker, was the
Captain of the Brean force and, on one occasion when a German
plane flew over low, and one of his men wanted to shoot at it,
shouted, 'For God's sake don't shoot, he'll drop his eggs on us' –
Shortly after it crashed.

The local paper carried many amusing cartoons of the Home
Guard, jumping the rhines and falling in, catching the bus with
Coggins running behind, (he was always late) and rushing to clear
the Brean Hotel.

MARCONI, 1874–1937

During May 1997 Brean celebrated the work of Guglielmo Marconi, 1874–1937, an Italian inventor who first experimented with radio waves in Bologna, Italy, when he was only 20 years old. He used Radio Waves shown in 1887 by Heinrich Hertz to exist, but no one believed they could travel sufficient distance to be of any practical application.

In Italy, Marconi's experiments were ignored, and because Marconi had an English mother, he moved to England to further his work. He lived at Coastguard Cottages, Uphill for some time.

One obvious application for wireless telegraphy was over stretches of water as an alternative to using submarine cables.

In May 1897 Marconi stayed at Lavernock Point, near Cardiff, and experimented for several months. On May 18th signals were made successfully between Flat Holm and Brean Down using kites and 4 strand wire.

Marconi worked with Sir William Preece, Chief Engineer to the Post Office, and the Post Office worked closely with Marconi and his experiments.

On May 7th Morse code pips were heard at Brean Down from Lavernock Point, a distance of 8.69 miles over water, a new record. In 1901 he received the first Atlantic signals in Newfoundland from Cornwall.

Brean celebrated the centenary of his work with radio signals from Brean Down, using the call sign GB100BD, and there was a Kite Flying demonstration. There were exhibitions of Marconi's work and a beacon lit on the Down.

Marconi's work laid the foundation for the development of radio communications and of broadcasting throughout the world. He died in Rome in 1937 aged 63. The following day every radio transmitter in the world was closed for two minutes as a unique tribute.

In 1910 the ship to shore wireless service made its first big contribution to the police service, when the notorious murderer Crippen was recognised on the SS Montrose which was crossing to America. The Captain radioed London and Crippen was arrested on landing.

FLORA AND FAUNA OF BREAN
The Flowers & Plants

Over the years and, with added caravan sites and tourists, some of the abundant flora of Brean has lessened or disappeared, but in Spring a drift of bluebells can be seen wild on many banks, and yellow evening primrose (nowadays much valued for their oil, and grown commercially for this) are found in patches on the dunes, and poppies of many types and shades make the roadside banks a brilliant picture. Many forms of *Mallow (Lavatera)* find the hot sandy soil and sea air ideal conditions for their growth, and some grow to tremendous size and height and flower abundantly. Some small mallow grow on banks and roadside, but the tree mallow and musk mallow grow both wild and in gardens, where they are prized for their large pink/purple flowers and easy cultivation.

Some plants were introduced to Brean to help stabilise the dunes and drifting sand. Bordering the sea shore is *Sand Couch*, found in the blown sand where it spreads rapidly, tolerating the salt in the sand. This then gives way to *Marram Grass*, a remarkable perennial grass rarely found inland, but of great use on sand dunes along the coast. It grows from rhizomes which creep far and produce a mass of fibrous roots which help to fix the shifting dunes. Marram Grass can best be seen on fresh blown sand, since when one lot of sand is fixed by its roots, as fresh drifting sand is blown up, new grass grows up through and repeats the fixing process. Thus 50–100 foot high dunes may be stabilised and then other growth takes over. The leaves are long and narrow and curl up in dry weather to conserve water but open up in moist air. The name is from the Greek meaning 'loving sand'.

Another plant first introduced to Brean as a sand stabiliser is *Sea Buckthorn – Hippophae rhamnoides*. A thorny shrub growing 6–8 ft. high with orange berries in the Autumn, this has certainly helped in stabilisation, and in some places is valued as a barrier between unwelcome incursion from the beach into private gardens. But it spreads underground, is very difficult to eliminate, can cause a nasty poisonous scratch, and causes havoc when it trails

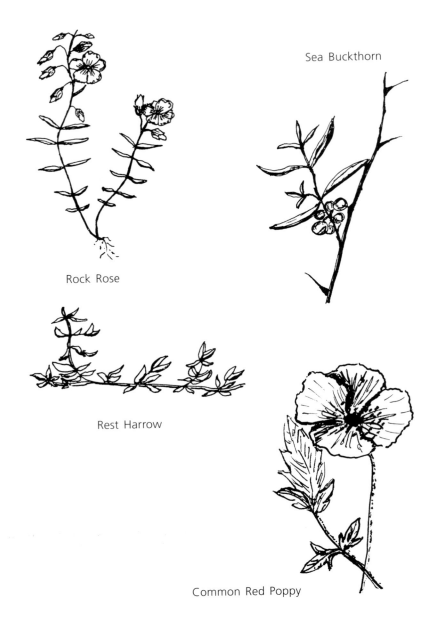

Sea Buckthorn

Rock Rose

Rest Harrow

Common Red Poppy

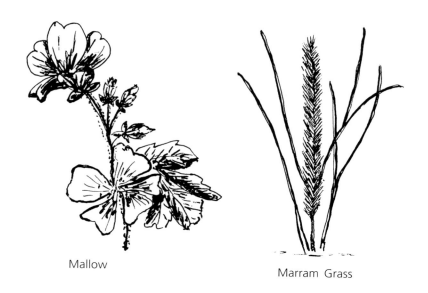

Mallow

Marram Grass

Yellow Flag

Rock Samphire

over and burrows under rights of way to the beach. In Autumn the orange berries cause quite a spectacular sight along parts of the roadside, and are a welcome feeding ground for the birds.

Along Red Road in May-July, *Yellow Iris or Flags* are bright yellow in the rhines on either side of the road. They stand 2–3 feet high with stiff erect sharp edges which can cut your hands if you try to gather them. They make a brilliant splash of colour along this pleasant, winding country road for which, from time to time, Sedgemoor has less pleasant plans.

A plant with a fascinating name is *Duke of Argyle's Tea Tree (Lycium Chinense)*, said to have been introduced by the Duke from China, and a not very welcome addition to most of the areas of Brean where it flourishes unwanted. It has long straggly green stems and sharp prickles which scratch the unwary and has tiny purple flowers, spreads rapidly, and can creep along the ground or grow to quite a height. It takes a strong dose of 'Roundup' to kill it.

Found on waste ground everywhere, but prolific on the sand dunes, is a perennial plant regarded by most people as a dangerous nuisance, *Ragwort*. This is poisonous to cattle and horses and should be pulled up and destroyed whenever possible. It has bright yellow flower heads on an erect branching stem. In Scotland it is called Stinking Willie due to its unpleasant smell when crushed. It is valued by some however, because it is the main feeding ground of the black and orange banded caterpillar which hatches into one of our day flying moths, *the Cinnabar Moth*, a red moth valued by environmentalists.

The bright black and yellow caterpillars are called by Somerset folks, 'them gurt maggots with football jerseys on'. Their bright colours warn off birds and are an unpleasant taste. A robin will usually leave them alone but, if it does try one, will wipe off his beak.

Brean Down has a wide variety of flora, particularly grasses. The naturalist, David Bellamy, in a television programme from the Down waxed lyrical about the plant life found there, and particularly the community grouping of such a wide variety. *Somerset hair grass, dwarf sedge, scurvy-grass and soft brome* are found there and sea loving flowers, *thrift and sea-campion.* On the Southern slope a *white rock rose,* which is very rare is found. This plant *Helianthemum Chamoecistus* is a common plant on calcareous soil, with a small yellow flower trailing on the ground among low herbage, but the white variety is unique to Somerset.

Also on the Down *Samphire* used to grow in large quantities on the rocky parts and was gathered and taken to Bristol market, where it was sold, and is cooked like asparagus and eaten with fish.

In August quantities of pink *Soapwort* comes out in gardens, banks and dunes. It is 18 inches to 2 ft tall, sometimes with single or double flowers. The name comes from the fact that, if its leaves are bruised and agitated in water, it raises a lather like soap and used to be used to remove greasy spots from clothes. Herbally it was used on the skin to cure the 'itch'.

The seaweed washed up on our beaches is of two types. *Laminaria* which grows under water, and *Fucus* growing on rocks above the tide. In Brean we mainly have knotted wrack and bladder wrack. Seaweed does not have roots, but clings to rocks with a 'holdfast'. Seaweed has a high iodine content essential in keeping our thyroid gland healthy, and used to make the strong disinfectant 'iodine' and, in the making of a gelatinous substance, ALGIN, used to stabilise foods such as yoghurt, ice-cream and make the smoothness of toothpaste and lipstick.

Some of the house names in Brean reflect the plants found there. *Marram Dune,* (opposite the Old Rectory), named after the prolific dune grass, and *Ononis,* (opposite Northam Farm). Frequently mis-called Onions, Ononis is Latin for *Rest Harrow,* a plant with flowers similar to Broom, but with pink flowers with one very large petal of a deeper pink than the other three. Rest Harrow grows on poor soil and flowers plentifully from June till September in many parts of Brean. Herbally it used to be used for toothache.

Warren Farm, the Warren, Warren Road, all remind one that the sea side of the road was a wild area of rabbit warren. Grass Road, an uncultivated track to the beach, Pinewood, a woody area with springs and ponds, and The Sands, Sea Mist, Tideways,

Beachwood, West Beach, Sandmore, Burrows, Shore Ridge, all reminders of the close proximity to sea, sand and shore.

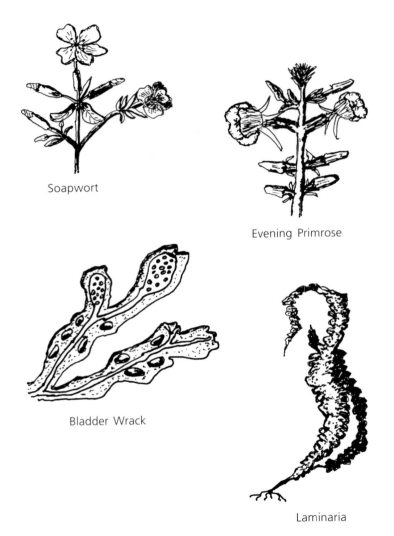

Soapwort

Evening Primrose

Bladder Wrack

Laminaria

THE BIRD LIFE OF BREAN & THE DOWN
The Fauna

The RSPB (Royal Society for the Protection of Birds) had a lease on Brean Down as a Bird Sanctuary between 1911–1952. For forty years Harry Cox lived, at least part of every year, as a warden of Brean Down, living at first in a wooden hut, and later in a more permanent home. He was a keen amateur ornithologist and protected the varied bird life which lived, visited or rested on the Down.

Birds thrived in the gorse and brambles, and enjoyed the seeds from the wild flowers which abounded, but fears of increasing uncontrolled undergrowth led to the introduction, first of grazing sheep, and later goats, and this led to the destruction of habitat and to the detriment of those birds which nested low to the ground. Skylark, Meadow Pipit, Willow Warbler, all need low cover to nest in. By clearing undergrowth the ground is made more accessible to walkers and holidaymakers, so increasing visitors will further decrease the nesting areas.

Harry Cox banned dogs from the Down, but there is now no such ruling. This too has led to a decline in nesting birds but is foolish on the part of dog owners, since a number of dogs have fallen to their death over the edge, usually chasing a rabbit or bird. This decline meant that in 1952 the RSPB withdrew their Bird Sanctuary status, and sold off their rights on the down without protest.

The war years were actually kind to bird life on the Down, it was closed to the public, though used by the Army, boffins from Birnbeck and the Home Guard, but, other than that, the flora and fauna were free to multiply. In fact badgers and foxes multiplied so well that fox shoots had to be arranged, and some badger extermination was carried out.

Many finches still visit Brean and can be seen in little flocks, swooping in on the seed heads in gardens and on dunes; householders who put out nuts in winter are well rewarded by many tits and finches which visit them.

Skylarks and linnets, which used to be found on the Down, are

Fox shoot on Bream Down.
Stuart Hicks, Phillip Frost, Frank Champion, John Perrett, Phil Champion.

rare now and the last Ravens nested in 1973, but there are reports of sightings and soundings of them again recently.

Ravens nested on the Down behind Brean Down Farm above the quarry, and these were closely protected by Harry Cox. Like the Carrion Crow they are useful birds for clearing up dead matter, but unpleasant tales are told of their behaviour towards sick or dying mammals.

Sheep sick with liver fluke after a long wet period lay dying in the fields by the Down, with Raven and Crow hopping among them pecking out the eyes and attacking the flesh, so badly affecting one farmer, that he had to move in and put the sheep out of their misery.

Another tale, vouched by Donald and Bert House, when they worked at Brean Down Farm, is of a ewe who was attacked and blinded by a Raven, but though blind, brought up her two lambs which, as they grew up, would nudge their mother to grass and

84

water. Sheep which rolled on their backs and could not get up might have their eyes pecked out, or else, as the sheep kicked, the raven would attack in the groin or armpit where there was little wool and rip open the body. They have their uses in eating up maggots on dead carcasses and clearing up rotten meat.

Magpies seem to be on the increase everywhere and raptors seem to increase, Kestrel and Sparrow-Hawk frequently hunt the dunes. The Kestrel hovers persistently over areas where it has spotted likely prey, whilst the Sparrow-Hawk makes lightening dashes over the dunes. The Peregrine Falcon has been seen hunting on the Down though they are not known to have nested since 1947. Shelduck used to be found in large numbers on the dunes, when there were rabbits and burrows which have now been replaced by bungalows and caravans, but they still breed inland round Bridgwater Bay. Bridgwater Bay is one of the largest moulting grounds in Europe for the Shelduck, where they feed on worms in the mud banks, but a great decline in breeding birds has been noted.

On the beach, flocks of Dunlin feed in the shallows and wet sand, they rise amusingly in a simultaneous wave as dogs or walkers approach, they take off, fly a short distance, then all land again and repeat this pattern the length of the beach. Sometimes from the dunes they can be seen in wheeling flight over the edge of the tide like a low floating cloud. Strangely the feeding habits of the sexes differ, males and females have different shaped bills, the males being short-billed, and the female long, requiring different type mud flats.

Migrant birds and rare visitors blown off track are sometimes spotted on the Down, being the first land resting site they may meet on flying from the Holms. Bewick Swan have been blown in in severe winters and the Hoopoe is a rare visitor, an exotic looking bird which has occasionally been seen at Brean and Brent Knoll.

The grey Heron is a fascinating bird frequently seen in the rhines along Red Road and between the fields. There is a heronry at Somerset Court, Brent Knoll. They stand long legged and long necked in the reed beds where it is difficult to distinguish them from their camouflage. They fish in the rhines and can be seen, head erect, swallowing fish, frogs and even eels which take a long time to go down the throat and neck. Thrushes used to be frequent in Brean. The noise of them smashing snail shells on the paths round the bungalows used to be an early morning waking sound, but thrushes are much scarcer now.

With decreasing habitat, increase in visitor pressure, changes in farming methods, and in Brean absence of farming, it is not surprising that bird numbers are falling. At least we are not hearing much about the barrage, no-one knew what effect that might have had on bird life, and the National Trust are going to look after the Down so Conservationists have some hope that bird life will be protected, and the Down remain largely unchanged, since it is the most likely site in Somerset for rare passerine migrants.

THE BADGERS OF BERROW & BREAN

Like the sheep on the Orkney island of Soay who have inherited a liking for eating seaweed, so the badgers of Berrow and Brean are unusual in that, for centuries, they have become beachcombers, and nightly wander along the tide line poking under the seaweed for marine insects and small marine life left behind by the tide. They cross several fields from their setts in the fields and banks, cross the road at well-marked spots, and proceed to the beach.

(My milkman once said he had had to draw up to allow a family of four to cross the road – and so through the dunes to the beach.)

At Brean Down where there is a large sett, they cross a field and go down the sandcliff to the shore. It is interesting to see what steep slopes they can climb without apparent difficulty. During their passage up and down the sandcliff they have loosened animal bones from the top layer, and also human bones from the early Saxon cemetery. I have picked up pieces of reindeer antler in the loose earth thrown out of their sett.

I have more than once found hedgehog skins turned inside out neatly by a badger, the rest of the animal having been eaten. During the long hard spell last winter when the beach was frozen, they used to scrape snow from the banks round the garden and eat bluebell bulbs, leaving their tracks in the snow.

Sometimes during the Autumn they give vent to a terrible yelling sound, the reason for which is not known as it happens out of the mating season.

(Sent by Audrey Kent from an original article written by her Mother, Mrs J R Naish, Rosemary Cottage.)

HARE COURSING

There is a strong tradition of hare coursing in Brean. The photograph shows a gathering of the hunt. This took place every Boxing Day at Brean Farm and this is pictured here. Followers and their dogs are here, a man holds a plank – 'the bridge man', whose job it was to build a bridge over the rhine so that followers could cross. The followers moved across the field in a line so the Flag man was at the end of the line to keep them straight. The 'Slipper' man released the dogs, two at a time – 'slipping' their leads. The owners were responsible for re-catching their dogs. Stories vary about Somerset hares. Loyal Somerset men say that they are the largest and strongest

Hare Coursing at Brean Farm
Note the Flag Man and the Plank Man.

in the country, but others that Irish hares are the best and that, sometimes, they were imported to make a better chase. (Perhaps they interbred to make the Somerset hare).

The judge rode on horseback to get a good view of the chase, and awarded points to the dog making the hare turn first. Local lads turned out as beaters and got a free lunch of bread and cheese and cider and, in the later days, £1.

Betting was heavy on the results and bookmakers were much in evidence. This turned a number of locals against the sport. When the hare had a sporting chance, and could run naturally, it was a good chase, and few hares were killed. As it became more commercial, hares were confused and driven towards the dogs and many people lost their taste for what was no longer 'sport'.

THE MODERN VILLAGE

Population figures for Brean show a steady increase in the size of the village:

1801	1811	1851	1901	1931	1951	1955	1956	1957
70	90	132	112	205	285	290	290	295

Gradually, as holiday making by the seaside became more popular, first campers and tents appeared on the dunes, and then people began to buy areas on the sea side where they built holiday bungalows, bungalows for letting and a few permanent homes. Consequently, in many cases, the deeds of these houses included the foreshore to the mean high tide line. It is therefore unusual, but much of the foreshore of the beach is privately owned, though subject to local bye-laws. Below this line is Crown Land and forms part of the Bridgwater Bay, a site of Special Scientific Interest (SSSI).

An extraordinary sight was a number of buses which people bought and made into holiday homes (before the days of the modern traveller) and before the vast number of static caravans which now fill Brean fields.

Enjoying the beach 80 years ago –
Mrs Marriage and Family in the tide at Goldrood.

Camping at Brean Down.

Boy Scouts at the 'Summer House', Brean Farm.

To counteract the blowing sand, marram grass and spartina grass were planted on the dunes. They grew in large masses and strong far-creeping rhizomes served to fix the blowing sand. Another imported plant was the Sea Buckthorn which spread extensively and also stabilised the dunes.

It is surprising to see how many trees do survive in this inhospitable area, willows, pine, sycamore, all flourish in some areas (though by their shape they all show the direction of the prevailing wind) and the dunes have increased considerably. Houses along by the turning to Weston had high tides washing nearly up to their walls, whilst now lawns, hedges, trees and added dunes now protect them from the sea. In some areas at least one extra 'dip' and dune have been added over the last 50 years. Many different ways have been found to protect properties from the beach and unwanted visitors. Some have built elaborate steps and gates, fences and posts, sometimes a heartbreaking process as winds, waves and vandals have destroyed them. Others have used the 'treasures' from the sea, old planks, gates, pallets to build multi-coloured sea defences and at least one property has a

In the mud on Brean Sands.

marvellous walkway up from the beach with steps, rope banister and tunnel through the buckthorn.

Brean beach has always been a good leisure beach because of the miles of flat sand from Brean Down through Berrow to Burnham-on-Sea. Low tide provides a large area for beach games, the sand is excellent for building sand castles and for sunbathing. The sea is warm and shallow and the low midday tides stay around for a long time allowing several hours of bathing, ideal for children and for sailing, water skiing and dinghies. But the tide recedes a long way over mud flats, and holiday makers must watch the tides. There are strong currents around the end of the Down. Unfortunately the mud base does make for a cloudy, muddy-looking sea and it is some way down the coast before clear water can be found. Much effort has been made to clear up the water, as well as the beaches, and to make it bacteriologically safe, but it is doubtful if clear looking water can ever be achieved.

Some years ago the Parish Council made a big effort to clear the mud flats of abandoned cars which had been driven out and lost in the mud. Despite warning signs, visitors still seem to find

91

it irresistible to drive cars out to the receding tide and then, to their dismay, find themselves stuck in the mud, an expensive adventure since a tracked winch has to be called from Weston to pull them out. Amazing reasons are given for driving out – one man wanted salt water for his fish tank so drove out, fish and tank in the back of the car. When the car stuck and the tide came in, not only the fish and the tank were filled with sea water, but the car also.

BREAN SEA DEFENCE SCHEME

Because of the Severn Estuary tidal range and prevailing westerly and south westerly winds, Brean is particularly vulnerable to storm damage and flooding from high tides whipped up by strong winds. Major floods were recorded in 1859, 1903, 1910 and 1926.

Sea defences of Brean were old and, in many areas, deficient

Rock armour sea defences, Brean Down, 1997.

and, in consultation with local residents, landowners and interested organisations, the Environment Agency put forward a £2.15m. Sea Defence Scheme. In view of threatened global warming and the low sand levels in the Brean Down area, with danger of future flooding, a programme of 'rock armour' sea defences was adopted. Before the scheme got under way, areas of the beach near the Down were dug as part of an archaeological dig, since previous digs had revealed features from Iron, Bronze and Roman periods on the Down and at its foot. Following this investigation the new defences commenced.

A line of sea wall was still in existence at the top of the beach, and it was decided to set the new line of rocks, 1.4 km. long against this. Rock was quarried at Cheddar, 18 miles away, and brought by five specially strengthened lorries to the site. These made up to six journeys a day, rumbling through Berrow and Brean and, if the tide and sand conditions were right, returning empty along the beach for the next load. Rock chosen was limestone to match the carboniferous limestone of the Down and, at peak times, 600 tonnes of rock were delivered in a day. The rocks were stored on the beach near where they were to be placed, but first shingle and clay were excavated and moved away from the placement area. Then a layer of geotextile was laid to provide a permeable membrane, and the rocks placed individually upon this, two layers deep, forming a band of rock armour about 10m. wide. This work was carried out in two phases to avoid the holiday season, between February and March 1996, and September and May 1996–1997.

The clay which had been removed was taken to the banks of the River Axe where river bank strengthening also has taken place. Shingle was replaced between the rocks, and walkways placed at intervals along the emplacements to caravan sites or houses. Heavy new floodgates were installed in 1997 to replace the stopboards at the top of both slipways, one at the Cove and the other at the public car park entry. The scheme was approved by the Environment Agency's Somerset Local Flood Defence Committee and grant-aided by the Ministry of Agriculture, Fisheries and Food. Sir William Halcrow and Partners were the Consultants, and the work was carried out by Amec Civil Engineering Ltd.

An opening ceremony was held on September 19th 1997 to mark the completion of the scheme, and a memorial stone marks the occasion on the wall at the beach entrance.

CLEANING THE BEACH

Keeping this beach clean is a major problem for the village. The tourist industry is of great value both to the village and to Sedgemoor, and since the beach is the main attraction, it is essential that it is kept clean. As most of the beach, to the mean high tide line, is privately owned by the householders along the coastal strip, Sedgemoor is not responsible for beach cleaning and wardening, though they do make a contribution towards it.

This costs in the region of £27,000 a year for cleaning, disposal of litter, maintenance of litter bins, clearing of rights of way and the services of a beach warden. Money is raised by allowing car parking on a large stretch of beach at a nominal daily fee, and letting out concessions to pony rides, ice cream vans, amusements etc, and expecting a contribution from the main beneficiaries of the clean beach – the site owners.

Litter on the beach is a big problem, not so much the litter dropped as that brought in by each tide. Seaweed is natural to beaches but, unfortunately, it is often littered with wood, cans, vegetation and, worst of all, plastic. Some of this waste comes down river from the towns, but much of the plastic waste may have been in the sea for months, coming from shipping and even from America.

Mechanical cleaning has been considered, but worries are expressed about this, since machines pick up not only rubbish, but seaweed, and the top layer of sand, destroying invertebrate life and its habitat, and thus removing food for birds and fish. Also removing this top surface can add to wind blown sand, and it is important that, where possible, sand and seaweed removed in beach cleaning should be added to the dunes to help to stabilise them and prevent erosion – but this must be done without unsightly non-biodegradable litter.

Before electricity came to Brean, houses and holiday homes had oil lamps and later calor gas and, with no double-glazing, central heating or electric fires, most households collected wood from the beach. Most of the old residents were avid beachcombers, even to the extent of taking chainsaws down to saw up large logs and railway sleepers for firewood, and drag up planks, parts of boats and other debris to feed the fires, make garden seats, posts or garden ornamentation. Nowadays it is milk crates, road cones and plastic buckets and bowls. Little wood is scavenged but left to be cleared.

Sand yachting is a favourite sport on the beach and a club meets most Sunday mornings. Between the wars many young men in Brean built their own yachts which they sailed on the beach, made with old tyres, car seats and, even in one case, part of grandmother's wheelchair! Modern yachts are much more sophisticated, reaching speeds of 60 mph, but very dependent on the wind. Two main classes of yacht are sailed in this country: Class III with 7.35 square metres of sail and Class V with 5.00 square metres. The club at Brean runs taster days for people to come and try the sport, and experienced yachtsmen will help and teach, and racing championships also take place.

Horse riding too is enjoyed on the beach. Horses can be hired and people also bring their own animals down. There are many miles to be ridden, particularly pleasurable on fine winter days when grass rides may be too hard, and the beach is in great condition for a gallop.

Dogs too enjoy the beach, and it is one of the few beaches to allow dogs free running all through the year, a fact much enjoyed by most owners as well as the dogs, and most owners are responsible and clear up after their pets.

The main sport on the beach however is fishing. The cover of this book shows skimming for fish, or flat fishing, which many families used to do in Brean with home-made nets. They were made of two long crossed bamboo handles, with a curved metal plate at one end of each, which were pushed along the sand in shallow water. A large net hung loosely between the bamboos and beautiful flat fish were caught – dabs and plaice, and even skate.

The fish caught in the net signalled their arrival by flapping against the fisherman's' feet and legs and then the whole structure was lifted from the water and the fish removed.

The fishermen of Brean 'knitted' their own nets. These were made on wooden needles, the stitches were cast on with twine and then lengths of net knitted. Small needles were used for shrimping nets, and larger for catching flat fish.

Other fishing was done with nets fixed to lines of posts, and had to be visited as soon as the tide went down before the seagulls swooped and robbed the catch. Most of the fishing today is done by rod and line from the beach (beach casting). The fishermen dig their own lug worms, digging an area like an allotment patch about a foot deep where the worm casts can be seen on the surface of the sand. To catch cod a 'cocktail' of lugworm and squid is used.

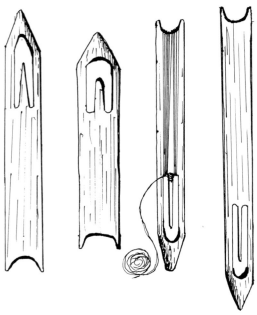

Wooden 'Knitting needles' & twine used to make or repair fishing nets.

The best months are September and October, catching the last of the summer fish and first of the winter. Flounders, Dover sole, Sea bass, Silver and Conger eels, Pouting are caught then.

In the autumn, Blonde ray, Skate, Codling and Whiting. In the winter months, Flounder, Codling and Whiting.

Fishermen go out early to dig their bait and then catch the incoming tide. They are a dedicated body of enthusiasts and can be seen on the beach in the foulest of weathers, fishing until well after dark.

Fishing competitions are held on Brean beach. The 3 B's (Brean, Berrow, Burnham) regularly hold competitions here, the October/November meeting being very popular and giving the proceeds to local charities. National Fishing competitions have been held here, these circulate around suitable venues in the UK. The Fosters National Competition held here attracted 300 competitors, entry fee is £3–4 but prizes are good.

There is some fishing from Brean Down, locals have their favourite spots and know the tides well. On the Southern side off the end of Brean Down is a deep water hole where salmon congregate before going up Channel, the Environment Agency watch this area closely since salmon fishing with nets here is illegal.

At one time thousands of sprats were caught off Sprat Point on the Down and was one of Weston's biggest sources of income.

HORSE AND PONY RIDES

Since 1949 there have been horse and pony rides on the beach. Jack Vowles, having a drink in the Brean Down Inn, and seeing a crowded beach, spotted a potential for 'pony riding'. He already ran licensed stables in Weston, applied to Brean Parish Council, and for £100 per year gained the concession for 20 horses on Brean Beach.

His son, John, joined him in 1960 and has been running the business there ever since. John had two brothers, also with concessions, and for some years had 20 ponies at Berrow, Brean and Brean Down.

From Mr Butt at Burnham they bought up three pony traps and

ran one of these from each point. These were very popular with the younger children. In Country and Western weeks which started at Pontin's in 1979 many riders come to John, and so he imported from America genuine Cowboy saddles and tack.

FAMOUS VISITORS TO BREAN BEACH

The long stretch of Brean and Berrow beaches has in recent years attracted a number of visits from television personalities and the filming of television episodes. A recent visitor to the beach, an avid Beatle follower, was trying to find the exact spot on the beach where in 1963 the Beatles were photographed. At this time they were at Weston-super-Mare, touring with Gerry and the Pacemakers, and were trying to penetrate the American pop scene. They spent a day on Brean Beach being filmed and photographed in Victorian beach attire. They also had a go on the beach go-karts. The posters, postcards and film were a huge success with the American market and created tremendous interest.

Pictures (unfortunately covered by copyright) identify the beach as opposite Shore Ridge, and the petrol pump as outside the fish and chip shop in Warren Road, which was then a general stores.

Gary Glitter and a party of friends have been to Brean on a number of occasions going to the Seagull and onto the beach to ride with John Vowles.

Ray Reardon, a frequent snooker player at Pontin's, was photographed on the beach on a horse for the 'Mystery Guest' in Question of Sport, and much excitement was caused in Brean when French and Saunders enacted a scene from 'Baywatch' on the beach.

David Bellamy has not only enjoyed the flora of Brean Down, but has also studied the wild life of the beach and dunes.

Princess Anne exercised her horses on the beach, when her outdoor riding was curtailed by continual frost and hard ground, but is reported as describing the beach as, 'naff'.

MERCURY COMMUNICATIONS

In 1987 Mercury Communications proposed the installation of a communication system linking the UK with the USA and plans to install a Fibre Optic cable from Brean beach across the Atlantic to USA and link with Japan and the Pacific basin. Headquarters for this plan were to be in Birmingham and Birmingham/Brean link was to be by underground cable.

The Mercury building is at Windmill House, Coast Road, and a submarine cable was laid underground and undersea across Brean Beach and across the Channel. Work was conducted between 1987–1988. This caused much entertainment on the beach, when many residents turned out to watch the laying under the sand of the Atlantic cable.

THE BARRAGE

In 1978 the Government set up the Severn Barrage committee to investigate the feasibility of a tidal barrage across the Severn Estuary in order to generate electricity. The recommended line for this barrage was from Brean Down to Lavernock Point. This caused much concern in Brean. The damage it would have on Brean Down. The effect on the village and, indeed, upon the actual location since reports varied considerably, and proposals placed the vicinity of the landfall 'somewhere within 6 miles either N or S of Brean Down.'

Obviously such a location would cause tremendous social upheaval: Compulsory purchase of land, construction chaos, disruption of village life and the tourist industry, and the effects on the infrastructure. No one seemed able to predict the effect on sea levels of Bridgwater Bay if the Barrage were built. There was possible destruction of the SSSI in Bridgwater Bay.

By 1986 the Severn Tidal Power Group, a consortium of companies, had still not put in a feasibility study but indicated that there were insurmountable difficulties if the Barrage were from Brean Down to Lavernock. The financial viability also was of great concern.

In 1987 further discussions were planned and phase 2 was to be 18 months-2 years, involving liaison with local and district councils. Work had still not started on design of turbines, grid distribution etc. Still no conclusion was reached as to exact location, and no decisions made as to provision of roads.

The new Millennium is now upon us. No barrage. No talk of it in recent years and financial requirements must now be astronomical.

BREAN DOWN IN THE TWENTIETH CENTURY

In the early fifties there was great concern as to the future of Brean Down and the Fort. Following the death of Mr Harry Cox who had been Warden for many years, Weston-super-Mare Borough Council were anxious to acquire the land and its rights which were regarded as a tourist attraction for Weston. In 1950 the Borough Council purchased four acres of the seaward end of the Down, including the Fort and a right of way over the Down for £1,500.

Weston hoped to purchase the remainder of the Down, though many Council members were worried at the proposed cost of £3,000, a 2d increase on the rates. They approached the Royal Society for the Protection of Birds (RSPB) to acquire the Society's interests in the Down, since they no longer considered it of interest as a bird sanctuary but the approach was ignored.

The owner, Mr Wyndham, was unwilling to sell the freehold of the land as he was anxious that it should be preserved as an open space, and not commercialised in any way. He finally agreed to sell to Axbridge Rural District Council at a price of £3,000, and with a covenant hoping to ensure its existence as an open space, – 'All that piece, or parcel of land known as Brean Down, in the Parish of Brean, Somerset, 159 acres. No. 179 Ordnance Survey map, together with all rights and interests, and all land lying between boundaries of property and high water mark as an open space.' Axbridge were delighted by this purchase and, as a splendid gesture, announced that they would 'present it to the Nation as a Festival of Britain gift'. Brean too were very relieved at this purchase since, as Brean Councillor Morley Hicks said, the Parish Council feared that if Weston bought the land, it would be part of commercial exploitation by Weston and without consideration of rural feeling.

Purchase of the Down by Axbridge included a covenant stating – 'Not at any time hereafter shall the said property be used for the carrying on of any trade or business or public entertainment, or for any purpose other than as a public open space'.

'Common seal of Rural District of Axbridge.'

The land was to be maintained in perpetuity in its natural state with reasonable facilities for access by the public, on foot. After purchase, the land was to be vested in the National Trust and the RSPB surrendered their lease but the grazing rights of the tenant of Brean Down Farm were to be preserved.

In 1950 Sedgemoor purchased the Fort from Weston-super-Mare, who were glad to be rid of it and the likely future costs of preserving it, for the princely sum of £1.00. But Sedgemoor did little to preserve it, or keep it safe, for the increasing number of visitors to Brean walking the Down and visiting the Fort.

Various parts of the Fort were demolished in the 1980's to clear away eyesores and dangerous areas, and later the roof of the barrack block was removed and walls were capped for safety.

In 1993 Manchester University Environmental Studies Group worked with Sedgemoor District Council to undertake a feasibility study to consider the future of the Fort. In 1996 it was decided that the full scheme should be a part of a bid to the Heritage Lottery Fund.

This caused tremendous controversy, splitting the village, parish council, residents association and received tremendous publicity in local papers, the national press and T.V.

Sedgemoor, as legal owners of the Fort, had a statutory duty to make the site safe, to ensure public accessibility and to maintain the Fort as a Scheduled Ancient Monument.

The first meeting in the village gained some support, but subsequent plans alienated many people, residents, visitors and many associations, such as the Mendip Society, the Council for the Preservation of Rural England and Brean and Berrow Residents Association.

Plans included management of the site, provision of an Interpretation Centre and residential accommodation and warden's flat. In order to make this a viable proposition, a café and shop were to be opened, ticket control, toilets and replica guns, shells etc. be placed to interpret the atmosphere of the Fort.

In order to make this financially viable, it was obviously necessary to greatly increase the number of visitors to the Down, and to provide transport for elderly or disabled visitors.

This aroused much fury. 4,000 signatures against the plan were collected, erosion of the Down, increased vandalism, added traffic in narrow approach roads, car park problems, destruction of wildlife, increase in vehicular traffic to service the Fort, were all quoted and public figures, such as David Bellamy, all spoke against the plan. Forefront of the objections, however, was the damage which would be done to the only tranquil, wild, natural place left in Brean or as the National Trust were quoted as saying, 'Brean Down is one of the landmarks of the Somerset coast. Today it provides a quiet place to walk, a downland setting in miniature between the busy resorts of Burnham-on-Sea, Berrow and Brean with their attendant caravan sites'. Only limited support was offered by the National Trust, Somerset Nature, Weston-super-Mare RDC and certainly no financial aid. Sedgemoor purported to have £40,000 available to tidy up and make safe, but the project would require another £710,000 to complete, and an estimated income of £85,000 annually to maintain.

The National Lottery turned this application down. Many doubts were expressed as to flawed financial figures, local non-support and lack of other financial backing. It would appear that a solution may be at hand, acceptable to most. The National Trust have co-operated in a 2nd Lottery bid being placed and agreed that, if this is forthcoming, Sedgemoor will use this to make the

Fort safe and in a secure state of repair. The National Trust will then purchase it for £1.00, thus owning the Down and the Fort which they will maintain in perpetuity for the nation. The Trust will obtain £440,000 endowment, much of it coming from Coastal development and preservation schemes. Enterprise Neptune and this unified trust will give inalienable rights, whereby the Down and Fort can never be developed and become a commercial enterprise.

This would appear to be the best possible solution, today in 1999 a 2nd Lottery bid has gone in, Sedgemoor will have to honour its pledge to make safe and secure the Fort and William Wyndham's covenants, requiring that the Down be 'preserved as an open space and not commercialised in any way' will be honoured.

In August 1999 it was announced that the new Lottery bid had been successful and £324,000 had been granted to repair and make safe the Fort. When Sedgemoor has honoured its promise to carry out this work, the National Trust will take over.

VILLAGE ORGANISATIONS — 2000

The modern village shows many changes particularly in the last 60 years. From being a small seaside farming village, visited by a few day trippers and campers, most of the farms have ceased to farm, the resident population has increased and the holiday trade now takes over the village.

Many holiday visitors, particularly from Bristol and Birmingham, having stayed in Brean, perhaps for a number of summers, have moved into Brean in their retirement. So, in common with much of Somerset, there is an elderly population. This resident population is approximately 550 but in the peak weeks of summer, with thousands of caravans and Pontin's holiday camp, this has been estimated as rising to 35,000. It is quoted as being the second largest caravan area in GB, second only to Skegness.

This makes the village a totally different picture from winter to summer. In summer many small shops open, stalls appear by the roadside, markets, car boot sales flourish, beach entertainments, car parking takes place on the beach, and fields, which used to be farm fields, are filled with static and touring caravans. In winter the village associations come into their own and, whilst they mostly don't close down in summer, many residents are too busy to attend.

There is an active Parish Council of seven elected members, who meet on the first Monday of every month, and deal with many problems, large and small, which arise in such a diverse village.

The Brean & Berrow Residents Association publishes a monthly magazine, 'Coastline', which keeps all its members up to date with village news from Brean and Berrow, and takes a strong view regarding many issues which affect the residents. Coastline Players are a drama group who meet regularly, and are mainly known for the well-established pantomime they put on each year.

The WI are active and, though their numbers fell a few years ago, are now back to strength.

Brean Social Club meet regularly and, as their name suggests, have plenty of social activity.

All the Associations meet in the Brean Village Hall, which was built on the site of the old village school, and which is run by a management committee representing all the Brean organisations.

The Lottery has been good luck for Brean. Coastline Players received a grant for essential lighting and sound equipment, the village hall received £5,000, which was spent on re-equipping the kitchen with new cupboards, cooker, fridge etc. £2,500 was granted to start an Over 60's Luncheon Club as part of the Help the Aged Lottery Grant. This meets twice a month when 24–30 sit down to a 3-course luncheon, and this year £2,400 has been received, again from Help the Aged, to run a Line Dance Group which meets every FRIDAY.

Now with news of £324,000 to preserve and make safe the Fort on Brean Down, it is hoped that Sedgemoor will spend this money wisely and hand over to the National Trust an interesting Ancient Monument fit and safe to visit, with years of neglect put right, and the essential tranquillity of the Down safeguarded for future generations.

BREAN CHURCH — REVD STAFFORD LOW

St Bridget's continues to serve the needs of the parish in Brean with regular Sunday Services and occasional offices. Weddings are infrequent with one or two a year on average with the consequence that the original register, started in 1846, is still only half full. With the extension of the churchyard a few years ago burials will be able to continue for quite a few more years but – as one would expect in an area with a large retirement population – funerals exceed both weddings and baptisms. Much time and effort is spent on maintaining the church and churchyard so that it can remain available for all to use and is kept open during the summer which, from the comments in the visitors book, is very much appreciated: 'An Oasis from the storms of life' is how someone described it.

The Church is now in the process of laying down a car park to avoid the chaos caused by parking on the road during the summer months, and is looking for sponsors to add to the three bells in the tower giving the ringers a challenge beyond 'three blind mice'.

Since the inception of the Local Ecumenical Partnership with the Methodist Church in 1988, the churches join together for a monthly united service and share the Songs of Praise services during the holiday season. They also jointly arrange the harvest suppers, Christmas lunches and Christian Aid activities and a number of social functions throughout the year.

It is when you walk down the path to St Bridget's and when someone asks you why there is a moat around the church that you realise how significant the sea and the sand is in Brean. In former times one would have been able to stand at the church door and look across the Bristol channel to Wales but, thanks to the sand dunes, the church has some protection from the wind, even if that same sand blocks the channels and causes the church porch to flood regularly. I wonder what people will say about the church in another millennium?

BREAN METHODIST CHURCH — HARVEY ALLEN

In the mid 1980's, witnessed by the whole village, Brean Methodist Church entered into a formal ecumenical covenant with St. Bridget's Church. The covenant, which is renewed every seven years or so, calls on the churches to worship, study, enjoy social events and serve the village together.

But even though it is committed to its links with St Bridget's, the church also cherishes the support it gives and receives with Methodism. It is part of the Weston-super-Mare circuit of churches (which includes Burnham) and the emphasis that Methodism places on lay participation means that its members can serve at circuit and national level. The church provides an alternative style of worship, a Sunday School was started informally in 1998 and midweek worship is also provided once or twice a month.

Over the years, members of the congregation have played a full part in the running of the village, whether on Parish Council or Residents Association, or in the social clubs that exist.

The church changes and will continue to change. In recent years improvements have been made to the building both at the back, where a better entrance hall and an enlarged kitchen area was constructed in the 1980's, and more recently, at the front where a new porch was created and a ramp built for wheelchair users.

BREAN PARISH COUNCIL — A J HAM – FORMER CLERK TO THE COUNCIL

In the Millennium time scale Parish Councils are a very recent innovation only developing their role in the last Century, as a vital part of the Local government scene as we know it today.

In the early days of the 20th Century most 'local government' rested either with the Squire or vested in 'the Vicar and Church-wardens' as the local embodiment of 'the Church'. Many of modern day services are derived from these roots. The Church was often responsible for education in villages, and the Poor

106

Laws made some provision for what we now know as 'social services'.

The Local Government Act of 1894 sought to rationalise and organise Local Government in a democratic form taking various shapes in different parts of the country. County Councils were set up and Rural and Urban District Councils established, and the option was given for each parish to establish a Parish Council. Many Parish Councils in the locality started at this time. Brean, however, was not established until the 1930's.

Although the 'lowest tier' of modern Local Government, Parish Councils play an important role in the life of any neighbourhood, various pieces of legislation have strengthened this role. Parish Councils can levy Council Tax to pay for its services – although Brean is unique in that it never has – have to be consulted on all planning applications placed in their areas, and have to account publicly for their income and expenditure; to name but a few.

Probably of more importance is the role a Parish Council plays in lobbying District Councils, County Councils and even national Government for the provision of facilities and services. Over the years Brean has been particularly active in this respect, having taken the lead in the provision of street lighting throughout the village, a sewerage scheme in the village, the provision of the Brean Village Hall, and the improvement of the road and provision of pavements throughout the majority of the village.

BREAN & BERROW RESIDENTS ASSOCIATION

The Association was formed in 1976 and was the Brean and North Berrow Residents Association, only recently has it become the Brean and Berrow Residents Association, and indeed a number of 'Coastline' are distributed in Burnham, not only to advertisers, but also to people who lived in Brean and have moved, or to those who have a particular interest in Brean.

The affairs of the Association were first published as a news-sheet, at first issued free of charge, but later in 1978 £1 a year was charged. The aims of the Association were given as:

'To make Brean & North Berrow a better place in which to live'. The first Committee is given as:

Chairman – P Ross, St Annes, South Rd.
Treasurer – A Vowles, Thorny Pen, Coast Rd.
Secretary – J Goodes, The Sands, South Rd.
V Chairman – J Griffen, Stoney Ash, Coast Rd.
Committee Members:–
C Lodge, Sunningcrest, Coast Rd. (Newsletter).
H Strong, Marram Dune, Church Rd.
L Holloway, Green Tiles, South Rd.
H Allen, Thornberry, Church Rd.
J Hazell, Sandpipers, Coast Rd.
Roger Short, The Old Rectory, Church Rd.

It is amazing to see the problems which beset the Committee twenty three years ago – very similar to today's – and little improvement. Beach cleaning – volunteers filling black sacks. 'Plenty of sacks but few volunteers to fill them. Thanks to Hugh Harris and his son, Jonathon'.

Policy Plan 1978. Agreed that all the seaward side of the dunes from Ativo to Mendip View should be residential, around the Church should be open space. There was considerable disagreement for and against using Red Road as a rear access route.

A series of village personalities were written up; Mrs Wormald, Mrs Strong, Miss Marriage, Mr and Mrs Rees, Mr Barry Allen, Mr Peter Ross, Mrs Vowles.

Shortage of police was evident, motor cyclists causing problems on the beach, speeding through the village and disturbance at weekends. Agitation for a footpath along the 'Southfield Narrows'.

An application for development of the Glebe Land was turned down, a charming letter from the Bishop of Bath and Wells was received, who agreed with the comments made and supported letters to the Land Agents and Diocesan Finance Office. The area has been designated as a possible play area.

In 1977 a party was held to celebrate the opening of the Village Hall, decorations by Judy Allen and Margaret Hicks, two flowering cherries were planted outside the Hall. An application for a small gauge railway to run from Uphill Ferry to Squires Gate, and then connected with an 'Edwardian' style bus to run along the beach was discussed.

The Committee was unanimously against this, and the hundreds of people it might attract to the Down and the village.

In 1978 there was a call for a Beach Warden to be responsible for enforcing the bye-laws and controlling the beach car park. First talk of the Severn Barrage was made. Continual requests for a children's playground in the village were made. The question of Life Guards on the beach caused much controversy. Many appreciated their presence, but others objected to their noisy loud hailers, washing hung out to dry, speeding of vehicles and rattling of collection boxes. The Parish Council withdrew permission for the Life Guards to collect money on the beach, and so they withdrew their services.

With the advent of a new Secretary of the Association in 1979, Mr Harvey Allen, the Association decided to widen its aims.

'To seek to preserve and encourage the community life of the village area' Continual trouble with street lighting. SWEB promised to install new light switches. *1980*. The issues this year were noise and hooliganism late at night. There was great strength of feeling at the struggle we have to maintain a decent standard of living for residents. Garish signs and stalls were criticised.

1981. Street lights 'the situation is both frustrating and appalling. We seem to be ignored in favour of other places with more clout'.

1982. A flourishing youth club existed under the care of 'The Grove Family'.

It was 1984 before Coastline achieved a cover, though the single page had increased to six to eight pages and adverts were accepted for the first time. Also the first year of the Festival of Talents.

Considerable trouble was caused by fishing competitions. Cars on the beach and in the children's play area, litter, using the dunes as toilets, were all blamed on the fishermen.

Berrow – considerable worries re erosion on the dunes, horses on the dunes and footpaths.

Continual requests for more police presence. Lack of footpaths. Congestion on market days.

The possibility of the siting of the Severn Barrage at Brean caused tremendous discussion both for the Residents Association and the Parish Council, many fears being expressed concerning lack of public consultation and the ecological impact such a scheme would have.

Also very controversial was the Sedgemoor Plan to develop Red Road as an alternative route into Brean, and this caused much lobbying of the Parish Council and parishioners.

Equally contentious were the Parish Council's plans to replace the gabions at Squires Gate and many arguments, and even a court case, was held before this matter could be settled.

The Sedgemoor Plan and Lottery Bid for repair and development of the Fort at Brean Down, including a café, residential accommodation, interpretative centre, vehicular access caused great uproar, the Residents Association were mainly against the scheme, and certainly doubted its financial viability and were against its environmental impact. Fortunately, after much lobbying, the Lottery turned down the application and then a much modified scheme and sum of money were applied for. Only repair and safety measures would be accepted and then the National Trust agreed to take over management.

Much of the work of the Residents Association continues, building plans are studied, objections voiced to the Parish Council, the aim 'to encourage the community life of the village' continues with Luncheon Club, Line Dancing and the production of Coastline magazine.

Coastline has continued to be the most important channel for information in Berrow and Brean. Over 400 households now are members of the Association and receive copies. It is now on a professional basis as befits the size of its distribution. We pay to have Coastline typed and printed and seek advertising in order to afford this, but our deliverers are still volunteers, so not everyone gets their copies on the same date, illness, holidays, sometimes cause delays.

Both Brean and Berrow Parish Council report their meetings,

and greater accord is now felt between the Association and the Parish Councils, though of course the Residents Association is still ready to press the case of its members whenever it feels the need.

During its lifetime Coastline won first prize and a cheque for £100 in 1988 for the best Newsletter in the 'Village Ventures' competition, and in the same year, the Parish Council won a European Year of the Environment Award and £300 for its initiatives in village and beach cleaning.

THE COASTLINE PLAYERS

A meeting was held on 22nd October 1985, opened by Bill Martin, to form a group. Interested in various types of productions, the following were then elected to form a Committee.

> *Chairman* – Walter Godwin
> *Secretary* – Pat Plimley
> *Treasurer* – Bill Martin

And Don Crook – very experienced in Amateur Productions – as Producer. Hence to be called 'The Coastline Players'.

Aims to promote and foster Entertainments, Revue and Old Time Music Hall. Membership was £2. Starting with seventeen members.

The Coastline Players are self-supporting with Fund Raising Nights of Chicken & Chips, Disco, Skittles, Tombola and Old Time Music Hall and Pantomimes. Our Revues have helped to pay for new curtains, several spotlights, a piano, and stage extension. Next on the list will be new sound equipment.

In recent years we have produced Pantomime only. We have not forgotten our ability to produce a good revue. With increased membership we hope to do this again. During the summer months the Coastline Players have held a number of Treasure Hunts and other social events.

The following is an article printed in SPOTLIGHT, April 1999, the magazine of the Somerset Fellowship of Drama.

'SPOTLIGHT ON . . . COASTLINE PLAYERS

Another Panto season has come to an end for Coastline Players, six performances at Brean Village Hall of Sleeping Beauty, after months of exhausting rehearsals, plus the aftermath of clearing up and dismantling the stage., 'was it ever worth it'!

Well, as usual, it was performed to a capacity audience each night. The hall seats only 80 persons with the stage extended, so tickets are very hard to come by. General opinion was that this was the best ever show (this is said every year) – how will we ever improve next year?

Each year there is an award presented for the most improved performance. It is called The Don Crook Award, and this year was presented to Joan Hart for her excellent performance as Carabosse, the Wicked Witch. (Well done Joan!) Don Crook was the originator of Coastline Players in 1985 and the award is judged and presented by members of his family.

A forerunner of Coastline was BATS. (Brean Amateur Theatrical Society). This group was interested in putting on sketches etc., but Don who was an accomplished actor, pianist and producer, felt we could go further and arranged short plays, old time music halls, Noel Coward Reviews and eventually the first pantomime, Dick Whittington, in 1987. I think the whole village turned out and thoroughly enjoyed the local jibes and hand-made make-do props. Some of those original members still take part in some way, and we now have some of the children who enjoyed those earlier shows, performing themselves.

The name of Coastline Players derived from Brean and Berrow being coastal resorts and, although inundated with holidaymakers in the summer months, when the idea of putting on a series of weekend shows was tried, it did not attract much interest from visitors. Perhaps we shall try again sometime! After all it was one of those extremely hot summers, and even the Playhouse in Weston-super-Mare only attracted around 12 people in their audience one evening.

For the last few years we have not managed a Spring or Autumn show. It is difficult when so many members are involved in the holiday trade and cannot spare the time required. Coastline Players do, however, try to meet each month during this period for social gatherings, such as barbecues, skittles and car rallies. We have around 25 members and many former members who come along to help, or socialise. We enjoy friendly rivalry with the Burnham-on-Sea Pantomime Society and support each other's shows. We are not so fortunate as to have a venue such as the Princess to perform in, so we have our limitations, and realise that perhaps we have outgrown the village hall. But we must not forget that Coastline Players are in the main performing for the villagers of Brean and Berrow and hopefully this will continue.'

Gordon Legg is Chairman of Coastline Players.

BREAN SENIOR FELLOWSHIP

In January 1978 the Brean Senior Fellowship was formed, this taking place in the Brean Village Hall, and it was agreed that meetings would be held every other Monday throughout the year at 2.30 pm to 4.30 pm. Various kinds of speakers would be invited and events held. As time went by, it became well patronised and by the early 1980's there was a membership of between 50–60.

Several days' outings were organised and, because of their popularity, it was voted to try a week's holiday. Bill Martin, being on the Committee at that time, was elected to organise same. Fourteen members all agreed to go and Falmouth in Cornwall was the venue. We all went in our own cars and it was a really excellent hotel. We were organised well and all had a very good time, so the next year we went to Sandown, Isle of Wight (20 that year), and the following year Worthing was the choice and 18 of us were there. Again we were fortunate with the weather and hotel. Unfortunately, owing to unfortunate accidents etc., the following year only eight booked to go to Jersey, but they obviously enjoyed it. Time went by with different day outings, one to Sidmouth, another to Forest of Dean.

In 1990, at the AGM it was proposed that the Club be renamed

'Brean Social Club', and, after a lengthy discussion, it was proposed and seconded that 'Brean Social Club' would be the new name.

The Club has its Christmas Dinner and Party in the Hall each year, and organises various Bring and Buy Sales or different types of daytime activities. Our membership has fallen over the last few years, but the Club is still being organised and run extremely well by the present Committee and we all look forward to the fortnightly meetings, need I say, for a chat and bit of gossip.

KNIT & NATTER CLUB

On coming to live in Brean in March 1980, it was a quiet country cum-seaside village and, as my husband Bill was still going to work every day, I had plenty of time to go out and find out different things that went on in the village.

By sheer luck, one day on one of my walks I met a certain Mrs Evelyn Wormald, who I knew in Bristol several years before. Evelyn is a very well known lady in the village, and has lived here since before the war, so she took me under her wing to make me feel very much at home. So she asked if I would join her ladies' club, called the 'Knit and Natter', normally known as the 'Knit Nat'.

This small club was under the care of Mrs Ray Rees, the landlady of the Beachcomber Pub. Being a very select band of ladies (12 in all), we met every Tuesday at 2.30 in the lounge of the Beachcomber after closing time of pub hours. Everyone had to either knit, do fancy work, paint, crochet etc., and we all used to thoroughly enjoy realising the lovely work that had been done in the week. I think I was the very privileged one to be there because I could only knit, so, of course, my other job was to make the tea and wash the cups!! Mrs Wormald is still with us, and still doing some lovely work, including painting, and she is 96!! Regretfully Ray is no longer with us, and the club disbanded about ten years ago.

In the years it was running the Knit Nat Club made Brean a

really happy and small country seaside life and Evelyn, I know, feels the same. To my knowledge, it was a very unusual little club, and each year they had their own little annual outing . . . and for one glorious moment our name and Club was talked about on Radio Bristol!!! Kate Martin.

BREAN WI

In the early 50's Mrs Chew was a well known figure in the village. She lived in the Manor, with husband and daughter, Rosemary, and she volunteered to organise and man a library for the village in the old Church Hall ex School − now Village Hall. Shelves were installed, books supplied and 'protected' by wire netting

Brean WI, 1965.
Left to right, back row: Pat Plimley, Ann McAinch, Sally Tuffin, Mrs Griffin, Mrs Jones, Bessie Puddy, Mrs Gilling.
Middle row: Mrs Hobbs, Evelyn Bagg, Mrs Pope, Mrs Silcox, Mrs Board, Mrs Allport, Mrs Champion, Gladys Harris, Mrs Wormald, Mrs Hatherall.
Front row: Mrs Coles, Mrs Rawlings, Mrs Florence, Mrs Harris, Mrs J Hicks, Mrs M Hicks, Mrs McNeil, Mrs Dibble.

doors! The Library was very popular, then Mrs Chew had another idea, by chatting up the ladies, regarding the advantages of the Women's Institute for Brean, she once again put the wheels in motion, organising three ladies from County Office at Taunton to come to a formation meeting. And so, on March 19th 1953, the Brean Women's Institute was officially formed with twenty-six members on the register, with Mrs G M Board voted to be the first president.

The format of a meeting has continued, almost to the letter over the years. We heartily sing Jerusalem, Apologies and Correspondence are read. Arising from, and any other business, discussed and sometimes momentous decisions made. The Speaker, next item on the Agenda, providing talks, slides, demonstrations, on the most varied of subjects. 'How to repair a fire-side chair', 'Work of a Guide Dog', (with models), 'How to protect your home and family when Atom Bombs fall' (1959). Then in 1974, 'Metrication and the Housewife' (when we learnt that more housekeeping money would be wanted).

After the Speaker a very welcome coffee and biscuit, with a Social Time to close the meeting, in the form of a Quiz Game or a chat! Each meeting there was a competition such as – 'A well-dressed Clothes Peg', 'Six Shortbread Biscuits' etc. Points awarded, then a Rose Bowl prize was presented for yearly winner. Jumble Sales and Whist Drives were held to raise money for Charities or good causes, but we have now moved up-market to Table Top Sales, but Jumble Sales were the biggest crowd puller and money maker.

Outings are one of the WI highlights with varied destinations:- Windsor Castle to a Canal Boat Trip.

It was soon realised that Brean WI was part of a very large organisation. We attended Group Meetings, with ten other WI's from nearby villages. Spring and Autumn Council meetings with representatives from all WI's in Somerset and finally National Meetings, for two days at the Albert Hall, London, where the rendering of Jerusalem was magnificent and all the ladies wore hats.

In June 1964 we moved from the Church Hall to the Methodist, because of the increased membership, almost fifty now.

In 1965 the highlight was an invitation (gold edged) from the Queen to a Garden Party at Buckingham Palace on May 31st to one member of each Institute. Voting took place and Mrs J Hicks was the lucky one to go. She wore a Cream *Crimplene* Suit, cream hat (large), cream umbrella, handbag and gloves. It was an exceptional day. Eight thousand, seven hundred and seventeen ladies attended – all in hats. Prince Philip was quite bewildered by it all but the Queen, being a Sandringham WI member was quite relaxed. The occasion was to celebrate the Golden Jubilee of the Institute.

Over the years many handicraft classes and exhibitions have been organised. A tablecloth was embroidered, showing a design of WI Badge, then a Banner for Brean was made and, much later, a patchwork cover for the new piano. All members did a few stitches to be able to say they had helped! Painting classes were also a firm favourite and produced some excellent artists.

A Drama Group has performed many well received productions, one melodrama, 'The Little Heir', never to be forgotten, 'Mrs Methusula' and 'Bus Stop', also a good laugh.

Also in the 70's a 'choir' was formed to raise money for Charities and Carol Singing round the village – this was much enjoyed by the singers, not to mention the mince pies and sherry at the end of the evening.

In 1958 the representative of Parish Council asked for our opinion on the 'goings on in the village', Development of Fish & Chip Shops and Slot Machines!! So degrading.

We were honoured to be asked to serve refreshments at the unveiling of the Parish Clock at Methodist in November 1972. Also to take part in 'Keep Britain Tidy', when WI ladies picked up the litter, complete with gloves, black bags and stick with a nail at the end, through the village!

Denman College is an interesting part of WI set up, and some of our members have attended educational courses there. Courses are varied. One of our members took a Welsh speaking course.

Each year we celebrate our Birthdays (WI) with a party or Theatre outing. We came of age in March 1974, and celebrated in grand style at the Beachcomber with 70 members and guests.

In 1977 the New Village Hall was officially opened and, by unanimous decision, we decided to have our meetings in the new hall, and two of our members joined the Management Committee.

Skittles, Scrabble, Beetle Drive and Coffee Mornings have always been most popular, not forgetting Faith Suppers, when each member brings food and we have faith there will be plenty for all. Our faith was never shattered.

An interesting meeting was held in 1981, 'Brean Olympics', when visitors and members joined in the fun. It proved difficult to keep the Olympic Torch alight, but then members divided into teams and colours. Egg and spoon race, blow football, darts were some of the 'games', and gold and silver medals were presented from the rostrum.

During the years we have collected money for a wheelchair for Kathleen Chambers Home for the Blind, also £350 at a later date for a raised scented garden. A cup, for the Sand Yachting International Event. A patchwork quilt was made by a collective effort in 1983 and £500 handed over to new Weston Hospital to 'Buy a Bed'. In 1983 a Mrs Weaver was presented with a pot plant, being the 50th lady to join the 'Wild Indians'.

Over the years we have had 'ups and downs' with our membership numbers, but now we are on the 'up'. Not quite ready for another pot plant recipient, but who knows what the year 2000 may bring, and perhaps this potted history of the last forty-six years will show how enjoyable the busy, enlightening, interesting Women's Institute member's life is.

Concluding with a mention of the excellent Presidents we have had over the years:– Mesdames G M Board, M Hatherell, J Hicks, H Strong, B Board, A McAinsh, D Rawlings, M Kerby, D Smith, B Willis, R Collins, C Phillips, J Hart.

Joan Hicks

BUILDINGS & SITES TO BE FOUND IN BREAN IN THE YEAR 2000

Many of the old buildings can still be found in the year 2000, in some cases altered almost beyond recognition, in some just a name by which to be remembered, and in others – just the same.

ASCOT, MERRYWOOD COTTAGE & ST MICHAEL'S — SOUTH ROAD

Merrywood Cottage was formerly called Olcote (Our little corner of the earth) and, together with St. Michael's, housed Brean House School. They were later occupied by Mrs Champion and Miss Harris.

Beside these houses, in the grounds of Northam Farm, is a house called *ASCOT* with the date 1865 on the front wall. Next to this is a stone building with an upstairs window. This was the carriage house and stables, and above it the hay was stored. Immediately behind Ascot is a thick stone wall, this marks an extraordinary Boundary line which seems to make little sense. On the sea side of the road Berrow ends at Whitburne (by the new roundabout) and Brean begins and extends along the coast side to Brean Down. But not on the other side of the road. Here Berrow extended through the site of Alicia – at one time a little school – through the back of the old Pontin's site, through the back of Brean Court, the road side of Northam Farm, behind Ascot, marked off by the brick wall, and up to the old site of the garage. The boundary then swings inland along the raised flood defence line, across the fields to Maitland Cottage in the old Weston Road.

Mrs Bagg (Evelyn Davis) lived with her parents in a cottage behind Olcote, and used to sit in the tree watching the children in Mrs Manning's school. When she got married she had to marry at Berrow, because the boundary line ran between the Davis cottage and Olcote. She was taken to Berrow Church in a horse and cart by Fred Champion. Mike Scott, living at Northam, had his banns called in 3 Churches. Berrow, because part of Northam was in Berrow, Huntspill, where Mary lived, and Brean, because part of Northam was in Brean. This boundary line only changed in the 1980's.

BREAN DOWN FARM

Many of the farms in Brean were probably built on the site of mediaeval forts. Brean Down Farm, it has been suggested, was of late mediaeval origin, but was re-built in the early seventeenth century. There is evidence to suggest that, at the time of the Warren on the down being damaged by poachers, and the case going to the Star Chamber, there were two houses, one on the sandcliff being the warrener's and the other – Brean Down Farm – the owner of the Warren. This is probably the house described as newly built when it was sold by Bond in 1637 to William Cann with 400 acres of land.

In 1861 William Wyndham is listed in Kelly's Directory as

Brean Down Farm – The Hawkings family.

being Lord of the Manor and he owned practically all Brean. The next owner listed is 1889 Jas. Frith, and then in 1894, Edward Champion.

By 1910 Jesse Hawkings and his family owned Brean Down Farm, having moved from Northam Farm. Jesse had a large family and a flourishing farm. A private governess was employed to teach the younger children in the schoolroom. The family were regular churchgoers attending morning and evening services at Brean Church.

Mr Hawkings was a member of Axbridge Rural District Council and on the Axbridge Board of Guardians. The farm kept pigs, fed on whey from cheesemaking, and killed and cured their own pigs, hanging up the hams in the kitchen.

Caerphilly cheese was made in large quantities and was of high quality, winning many prizes.

Two of the sons went into the Army in the 1914–18 War and in 1917 Edgar was wounded in France.

On a hot Sunday morning in 1917 Jesse Hawkings was ready to go to Church, but went out to visit his stock. First he visited the pigs and talked to his labourer, Billy Bence. Then he went to look at his pedigree bull which he had only had for 6 months.

Without warning, the bull charged the gate, breaking it off the hinges, and gored the farmer to death. The Dr was fetched but had to come from Burnham and the farmer had died at once. At the inquest it was ruled that he had been attacked by an infuriated bull, probably due to the heat of the day, but no neglect was attributable to anyone.

On June 14th 1917 – there was a very large funeral, since Mr Hawkings was well known and considered the best of friends and kindliest of neighbours. The village school was closed for the afternoon in order that the older children could sing in the choir at the service.

The estate was wound up quickly, 2 sons were in the army and the next, Tim, enlisted in the Worcesters. The other children were still at school, and so the family moved, and Brean Down Farm was tenanted by Mr Roland Frost.

Roland Frost continued farming and the tradition of cheese-

The Farmhouse Restaurant – Brean Down Farm.

making. He had 4 daughters, Ruth, Nan, Molly and Phyllis, and built beside the farmhouse a long tea rooms, running along the foot of the Down which his wife and daughters ran. (Before this they used to serve teas on the lawn of the farm).

The tea-room did good trade with people coming over from Weston on the ferry which landed behind the farm. They sold lunches and teas with produce from the farm and very good vegetables grown on the slopes of the down behind the café. It was famous for the glorious asparagus which was grown and which Mr House, working there for his uncle, well remembers picking.

THE BEACH RESTAURANT

In the 1930's Roland Frost opened the Beach Restaurant, now the Cove Café, on the site of the old thatched cottage. His daughters proceeded to run this as well as the Restaurant at the farm.

Behind the café at The Hump lived Mr Wildridge. He ran a fish, poultry and game business in Weston, but at Brean he bred and kept greyhounds. He had two men to look after them and raced them at stadiums such as Eastville. Mr Wildridge was a

Thatched cottage at Squires Gate – Brean Down.

Opening of Beach Restaurant – Cove Café, 1930.

great betting man and, as such, was also closely associated with hare coursing which regrettably became a much more commercial sport.

He tried to improve the rabbit stock on the Down and introduced some dark and some black rabbits to interbreed. A few black

Mrs Board's tea room and tennis court.

rabbits still appear in Brean, known locally as 'Parsons' – perhaps they are from his importations.

THE COVE CAFÉ

The new owner of the Café at Squires Gate was an ex-boxer, Mr Bill Osbaldeston, who had the house built next to the café. To build this, he employed an old man of over 80 who lived at Wedmore. Bill Osbaldeston fetched him from Wedmore each day and loads of large pieces of quarry stone were brought in. He used to break up these stones by hand and fit them together with incredible accuracy to build the walls. Bill also built the first ramp onto the beach. Old pictures show how much lower the beach is now than when it first ran from the thatched cottage. Bill also had a racehorse, 'Osbaldeston,' which ran locally and with some success.

BREAN GARAGE

Before the modern garage was built the old garage was on the opposite side of the road. It was owned by George Clapp and his son Burns. George was a well known character in Brean who only had one eye and wore a pink eye patch. He used to sit outside his garage smoking an old pipe and, if it rained, put a lump of seaweed in the bowl of the pipe to keep his baccy dry. Burns owned one of the first cars in Brean and ran a taxi service. The business is first mentioned in Kellys directory of 1927.

It was necessary to have a taxi if one wished to travel by train to or from Brean, because *Brean Road Halt* was about 2½ miles from the centre of Brean, close to the Weston Rd. near Hope Farm. It consisted of a wooden platform and iron shelter, one each side of the track. This was part of Brunel's GWR which came to Somerset in 1841 and was nicknamed God's Wonderful Railway. Strangely Weston-super-Mare which was growing fast did not want a railway to the Town, and only later a loop line was added.

Brean Garage.

125

There is a tragic story of George Clapp's parents, Albert and Elizabeth Clapp. They had lived in a cottage where the house 'Pattingham' now stands, but had moved to a cottage at Berrow.

Albert Clapp was a fisherman. On Saturday night, 28th September 1902, Albert set off for the beach to visit his fishing nets which were hung about a mile from his house. The tide was due in at 2.00 am, it was a dark night with thick fog. Albert would have set off between 5–6 pm and would have been expected back at 8.00 pm.

At the inquest, George Davis of Brean, stated that at 9.00 pm he saw Mrs Clapp carrying two lanterns setting off towards the sands.

Next morning Albert Clapp was found at high water mark about a mile from Berrow Church. The verdict was found drowned and it was stated that he had very bad eyesight and had probably got lost.

Mrs Clapp had not drowned, but had previously been diagnosed as having a diseased heart and, with the exertion and anxiety of searching for her husband, she had suffered a heart attack. George Clapp identified the bodies of his parents, Dr Wade having conducted a post-mortem examination.

The following song, 'On Berrow Sands' was written about the story.

On Berrow Sands
Music by Stephen Adams.—Words by F.E. Wetherly

A light wind blew across the bay
And round the stakes at sea.
The fisherman was old and grey,
With tottering steps went he.
'You'll watch the tide, dear wife' cried he,
And clasped her trembling hands.
'And hold a light my path to guide
Across the Berrow sands'.

The twilight wrapt the little town
And hid the stakes at sea;
The wind blew up, the mist came down,
As forth to watch went she.
'Come back to me, come back she cried,
And waved the flickering light,
But faster crept the hungry tide
And darker fell the night.

At day break, on the shining sand
There by the stakes he lay
She, with the lantern in her hand,
Lay lifeless up the bay.
O let them slumber side by side
To wake on heaven's blue shore,
Where neither mist nor hungry tide
Shall ever part them more.

BREAN DOWN HOTEL

Brean Down Hotel opened in Brean in 1932. Built by W J Pople
& Sons of Bridgwater, it was built on very modern lines with hot
and cold water in all the bedrooms. The tariff shown below
illustrates pre-war prices. There was much opposition to the
building of this Hotel from the Methodist Church and it was 3
years before they were granted a licence.

Tariff
August 4½ guineas per week. Other months 3½ guineas
Bed & Breakfast 7/6. Winter Oct-April 6/6
Daily Terms 12/- except August.
Lock up garage 1/-
Extras: Early morning tea 3d per person.
Meals served in bedroom 6d. Baths hot or cold 6d.

THE MANOR HOUSE

Despite its name the Manor was a farm not a Manor. The house had various tenants but was eventually sold to a family called Curry, who later moved on to Diamond Farm, selling out to a wealthy brewing family, Mr and Mrs Wethered.

Mr Wethered used to bring his wife and family to Brean for holidays. A week before they moved in, the servants arrived to get the house ready. There was a footman, butler, cook, kitchen maid and parlour maid. Another maid was employed to look after the upstairs and a between maid to help where necessary.

The outbuildings, where the Beachcomber now stands, were cowsheds. The big Hay house across the road was used for celebrations such as Queen Victoria's Jubilee in 1887 and the Relief of Mafeking in 1900. Mr Wethered built on quarters for servants. The Beachcomber became stables, with a coach house and two lovely black horses, and the Coachman lived above the coach house.

Mr Wethered was responsible for a great act of philanthropy, buying the land upon which the village school stood when it came up for auction in 1903, and then presenting the parishioners of Brean with it in 1909, so that the village owned this land when the school was knocked down and the village hall built.

PINEWOOD 1977

Development of this small estate started in 1977, described in the Residents Association newsletter as 'a distressing sight for tree lovers and those conscious of our lessening acreage of open land'.

In the late 20's the 7 acres of land now known as Pinewood was bought and developed by a Mr Hewitt. He built a house 'Doorn Kloof' and created a nature reserve. He was by nature a recluse and it is said that he witnessed the death of Emily Pankhurst when, as a Suffragette, she threw herself under a horse.

Few people got to know Mr Hewitt, though Arthur Davis worked for him in the evenings and struck up quite a friendship with him (when he died he left Arthur his gold watch). Much of the estate was fenced and inside was planted with trees and shrubs, flowers and bulbs and ponds dug and stocked with a wide variety of fish. He made many nest boxes and attracted many wild birds.

No badgers had been found in this area of dune previously, but these were introduced and are still found along this strip of dune and in Northam Farm. He drank only goat's milk, and kept a nanny goat which he stood on the kitchen table to milk each day.

When Mr Hewitt died Mr and Mrs Board moved to 'Doorn Kloof', but eventually this was pulled down and the estate sold to a construction company, and Pinewood developed. Hewitt Close reminds one of the original owner.

In recent years badger and fox have returned to Pinewood, the occasional squirrel is seen, wild flowers have returned and many birds come to the gardens, tits, wrens and finches and even woodpeckers are seen.

THE RECTORY AT BREAN

This is now called The Old Rectory and is a private house. It is now a large pleasant house, but in 1535 was only valued at £7.04.

Thomas Strong, the maid Sally Kerton and visitors with Ford model T outside the Rectory.

129

and by 1668 at £30. Since few of the old Rectors lived in Brean the Rectory was unimportant to them. It was 1849 before the Rector, Michael Terry, enlarged and improved the house.

It still remains much as it was for the last 100 years. There is still a gateway set in stone walls, steps down to the back door and kitchen, an arched doorway into the garden matching the Perpendicular style of the Church and a similar gateway from the garden to the Churchyard.

The greatest change is to the buildings to the right of the entrance. The old schoolroom, not a school but a Sunday School, the stables, carriage house, have all been turned into neat little holiday 'bed and breakfast' homes, self-contained but with breakfast served in the main building.

The garden still has many old fruit trees, but gone are the ducks, geese, hens, ponds, cats and tennis court.

The directory of 1889 gives the only post box in Brean as being in the wall near the Church. 'Cleared at 5.15 pm each day. Letters by foot post, from Bridgwater, via Burnham arrive at 10.00 am. The nearest money order and telegraph office is at Burnham.'

Church Road, Brean – the village Post Office, T'ween cottage and Chapel.

THE POST OFFICE

This is first mentioned in Kelly's Directory of 1935. The proprietor was John Ward and it is described as a Post Office and Grocery Store.

The only other shop also listed, MARS Cash Stores, Paris and McPhee – Grocers.

Pontins – Brean.

BREAN HOLIDAY CAMPS

BREAN SANDS HOLIDAY RESORT

The first camp usually referred to as Deans' Camp was in fact called Brean Sands Holiday Resort. It opened in 1935 but only ran until the outbreak of war. Started by Mr Leslie Dean, on the land where Pontin's now lies, the camp consisted of a number of small wooden chalets built by a timber merchant friend, George Harris.

The chalets were small, consisting only of living space, bedroom and washroom, and all the catering was in a big dining room and there was a large social room which village activities could also use. The camp was erected very quickly by George Harris and his men, only 3–4 months, ready to open for the 1935 season.

By 1939, when war broke out and people would no longer be able to travel on holiday, the Government commandeered the camp as an Army base. American troops were based there, at first used as a storage and mechanical repair camp, but later as a transit camp before the Americans went home.

Consequently, as this represented the final posting, no-one cared much about the state of the camp and the Army left it in a terrible state of disrepair and desolation, many of the huts being sold off around the village as garden sheds.

PONTIN'S – BREAN SANDS HOLIDAY CAMP

Mr Fred Pontin (now Sir Fred Pontin), working in Bristol for the Ministry of Labour, after the second World War, wished to start up a Holiday Camp – on the lines of the famous Butlin Camps of pre-1939 days, and had long searched the whole of Somerset without success, until one day he was told about an American Army Camp at Brean Sands which was to be vacated as the soldiers left for home in the USA. The Camp – a site of 27 acres, was a series of huts in a bad state of repair, with an original capacity of 198 beds, and it was as well he first saw it on a fine day.

After a weekend of thought he arranged to buy it for the cost of £23,000 and, as he had nothing like that amount of money, he formed a syndicate for himself, his family and his friends, in the sum of £25,000, and also borrowed the maximum amount of credit from four Somerset Branches of Barclays Bank Limited, with their Head Office in Bristol. He retained a 51% control.

This gave him the money to repair the Camp and to buy furnishings – beds, bedding, mattresses, and other items, from the Ministry of Works, at very little cost as so many such Camps were being closed down at the time.

The deal to buy Brean Sands was completed in April 1946, and the Camp opened to the public on 1st July 1946. Brean Sands Holiday Camp prospered. As money became available, so improvements were made – to the living accommodation and to the main buildings, and the success of Pontin holidays was assured.

Shortly after opening Brean Sands in July 1946, Mr Pontin found another suitable site to buy, Osmington Bay near Weymouth – purchased for £46,000, and in the next year Pakefield Holiday Camp, near Great Yarmouth.

By 1959 there were 9 Holiday Camps with full catering facilities.

Corals bought Pontin's in 1978, and Sir Fred Pontin retired from the business at this time.

Corals were then taken over by Bass in 1980 and, in 1985, it was decided to place Pontin's under the management of the Board of Crest Hotels.

In Spring 1987 the Company was purchased by a group of private individuals, led by Mr T J Hemmings who had previously been members of the Pontin's Board. The Company was run as a private operation until 1989, when 50% of the equity in the Company was purchased by Scottish and Newcastle Breweries, with an option on the remainder which was taken up at the beginning of 1990.

The Company now operated within the Leisure sector of Scottish and Newcastle which consists of Holiday Club Pontin's, a controlling interest in Centre Parc's, together with a Time Share Operation and 4 Star Hotel, known as Langdale, and 2 Holiday Club Internationals in Sardinia, a Travel Agency and interests in parcels of land both on the Continent and at home.

TRAVCO

We know of Pontin's and its predecessor, Deans in Brean, but few know that there was nearly another camp built here.

A London organisation, TRAVCO CAMPS LTD of Transport House, London, before the 2nd World War, bought the Manor House, Beachcomber, and surrounding lands, including four acres on the Weston road and twelve acres towards Turnborne.

This land and buildings were purchased in order to build a holiday camp for Labour supporters. As this could not be developed during the war, the land was rented to Philip and Hugh Harris for the princely sum of two pounds and ten shillings per month. For this they had to agree to keep hedges and fences in good order, use it to graze and pasture cattle, keep it free of weeds and all noxious growths.

The area of land being known as Home Croft and Brick Ground in Weston Road. In 1960, when it became obvious that they would not develop further, it was sold again. Mr and Mrs Chew bought the Manor House, Mr Morley Hicks and Warren Farm purchased the land. Mr and Mrs Chew had a bargain, £2,000 for the Manor House!

BREAN VILLAGE HALL

This building is on the site of the old village hall. It is on land bought and given by Mr Wethered in 1909.

At first when the old school closed it was used as a Library, run by Mrs Chew, with books guarded by wire netting. During the second world war the building now known as the 'church hall' was used as the Air Raid Warden's Post, and in 1953 for the inaugural meeting of the Brean WI. But the building and car park were getting in such a bad state of repair that it was finally knocked down in 1973.

The Parish Council had to obtain the land from the Charities Commission, and had to agree that the new hall should have seating for 100 and building work should be completed within seven years. It was purchased for about £2,000 and a dedicated party of Brean residents set about raising money to build a Village Hall. It was completed well before the seven years were up, and on March 19th 1977 the hall was officially opened by the Lord Lieutenant of Somerset.

Later extensions were made to the hall, and in recent years, Lottery grants have made possible enhanced facilities for Coastline Players and a refurbished kitchen. The hall now is very well used including weekend bookings by Brownie and Cub Packs who 'camp' there, sleeping on lilos in the main hall.

The Village Hall Committee is very active in promoting activities and fund raising in order to make the Hall one of the best in Somerset.

Demolishing the village school to make room for the village hall.